Slaver

This book considers the imp
British economic developme   ... the
restoration of the Stuart mor   ... era of the Younger
Pitt. During this period Britain's trade became 'Americanised' and
industrialisation began to occur in the domestic economy. The
slave trade and the broader patterns of Atlantic commerce contributed important dimensions of British economic growth
although they were more significant for their indirect, qualitative
contribution than for direct quantitative gains. Kenneth Morgan
investigates five key areas within the topic that have been subject
to historical debate: the profits of the slave trade; slavery, capital
accumulation and British economic development; exports and
transatlantic markets; the role of business institutions; and the
contribution of Atlantic trade to the growth of British ports. This
stimulating and accessible book provides essential reading for
students of slavery and the slave trade, and British economic
history.

KENNETH MORGAN is Professor of History at Brunel University.
His recent publications include *Fritz Reiner, Maestro and Martinet*
(2001), *Slavery and Servitude in North America, 1607–1800*
(2000), *The Early Modern Atlantic Economy* (edited with John J.
McCusker, 2000), *The Birth of Industrial Britain: Economic change,
1750–1850* (1999) and *Bristol and the Atlantic Trade in the Eighteenth Century* (1993).

New Studies in Economic and Social History

Edited for the Economic History Society by
Michael Sanderson
University of East Anglia, Norwich

This series, specially commissioned by the Economic History Society, provides a guide to the current interpretations of the key themes of economic and social history in which advances have recently been made or in which there has been significant debate.

In recent times economic and social history has been one of the most flourishing areas of historical study. This has mirrored the increasing relevance of the economic and social sciences both in a student's choice of career and in forming a society at large more aware of the importance of these issues in their everyday lives. Moreover specialist interests in business, agricultural and welfare history, for example, have themselves burgeoned and there has been an increased interest in the economic development of the wider world. Stimulating as these scholarly developments have been for the specialist, the rapid advance of the subject and the quantity of new publications make it difficult for the reader to gain an overview of particular topics, let alone the whole field.

New Studies in Economic and Social History is intended for students and their teachers. It is designed to introduce them to fresh topics and to enable them to keep abreast of recent writing and debates. All the books in the series are written by a recognized authority in the subject, and the arguments and issues are set out in a critical but unpartisan fashion. The aim of the series is to survey the current state of scholarship, rather than to provide a set of pre-packaged conclusions.

The series had been edited since its inception in 1968 by Professors M. W. Flinn, T. C. Smout and L. A. Clarkson, and is currently edited by Dr Michael Sanderson. From 1968 it was published by Macmillan as *Studies in Economic History*, and after 1974 as *Studies in Economic and Social History*. From 1995 *New Studies in Economic and Social History* is being published on behalf of the Economic History Society by Cambridge University Press. This new series includes some of the titles previously published by Macmillan as well as new titles, and reflects the ongoing development throughout the world of this rich seam of history.

For a full list of titles in print, please see the end of the book.

Slavery, Atlantic Trade and the British Economy, 1660–1800

Prepared for the Economic History Society by

Kenneth Morgan
Brunel University

CAMBRIDGE
UNIVERSITY PRESS

PUBLISHED BY THE PRESS SYNDICATE OF THE UNIVERSITY OF CAMBRIDGE
The Pitt Building, Trumpington Street, Cambridge CB2 1RP, United Kingdom

CAMBRIDGE UNIVERSITY PRESS
The Edinburgh Building, Cambridge, CB2 2RU, UK   http://www.cup.cam.ac.uk
40 West 20th Street, New York, NY 10011–4211, USA   http://www.cup.org
10 Stamford Road, Oakleigh, Melbourne 3166, Australia
Ruiz de Alarcón 13, 28014 Madrid, Spain

First published 2000

Printed in the United Kingdom at the University Press, Cambridge

Typeface Plantin Light   *System* 3B2   [CE]

A catalogue record for this book is available from the British Library

ISBN 0 521 58213 X hardback
ISBN 0 521 58814 6 paperback

Contents

Maps

Tables

Acknowledgements

The germ for this book originated in a paper presented at a colloquium on 'International Trade and British Economic Growth from the Eighteenth Century to the Present Day'. Sponsored by the Istituto Italiano per gli Studi Filosofici, Naples, this graduate seminar was held at the Centre for Social History at the University of Warwick in 1988. Some years later it struck me that the material covered in my paper was wide-ranging enough to fill a short book. The present study therefore offers a more detailed consideration of slavery, transatlantic trade and British economic development (1660–1800) than space permitted in my original paper. The book has benefited from the opportunity to discuss pertinent themes at the following international conferences: 'Eric Williams and *Capitalism and Slavery*: Fifty Years Later', University of the West Indies, St Augustine, Trinidad, 1996; 'Trading Places: Colonialism and Commerce', University of Queensland, Brisbane, 1999; and 'History of the Atlantic System, c. 1580–1830', University of Hamburg, 1999. Brunel University funded my attendance at some of these events. The University of Hamburg underwrote my travel expenses to Germany. I am grateful for this support. I also wish to thank Selwyn H. H. Carrington, John A. Davis, Peter Mathias, Horst Pietschmann and Chris and Helen Tiffin for inviting me to speak on these occasions. The former series editor Michael Sanderson made helpful suggestions about clarifying some technical issues for students unfamiliar with the intricacies of maritime enterprise. H. E. S. Fisher advised on several specialist points. David Ryden helped me considerably in the technical aspects of preparing the book for the press. Jacob M. Price has influenced my thinking on many issues covered in the chapters below, and I would like to thank him for staunch support over the years. On the home front, Leigh has unselfishly shouldered more than her fair share of childcare while I was writing the book, and Ross and Vanessa have done their best to prise me away from the word processor.

Introduction

The connections between slavery, Atlantic trade and the British economy between 1660 and 1800 are an appropriate subject for a book in this series, for Britain in the period under consideration witnessed the 'Americanisation' of overseas trade, the last years of a pre-industrial economy and the birth of the first industrial nation. British merchants, planters and politicians became more interested and involved in the growth of empire and transoceanic trade in the long eighteenth century. Gregory King's estimates of social structure showed that in 1688 England had a well-developed commercial sector consisting of merchants, tradesmen, shopkeepers, artisans and handicraftsmen – a more differentiated and extensive middling *CLASS* sector than in any other western European country (Mathias, 1983: 27). The existence of a strong commercial sector in the English economy by 1700 provided a strong platform for the impetus towards commerce with and settlement in far-flung territories. Overseas expansion was accompanied by the emergence and growth of plantation slave labour in North America and the Caribbean. As the British economy developed in the Hanoverian period, greater manufacturing and agricultural output was accompanied by a demographic upswing after c. 1740, technological improvements in coal and textiles and a burgeoning network of inland and overseas trade. It is therefore logical to enquire into connections between the growth of an Atlantic empire and the development of the mother country's economy in the period from the restoration of the Stuart monarchy to the era of the French revolutionary wars.

Fortunately, there is a considerable scholarly literature that includes vigorous discussion on the significance of slavery and oceanic trade in British economic development. The debates have been sporadic but intense, frequently unresolved but important enough to leave a strong resonance in the historiography of the subject. These discussions have multiplied over the past twenty years or so. The fact that many contributions to the topic are scattered in articles and chapters of books affords the opportunity for a synthesis such as the present effort, which aims to keep students and teachers abreast of the leading debates and which, I hope, has something of its own to say. This, then, is a contribution to an ongoing discourse about the economic benefits of imperial trade and slavery. It seeks to provide answers to three broad questions: what were the financial rewards from slavery and Atlantic trade in the British Empire in the period from the mid-seventeenth century to the turn of the nineteenth century? To what extent did those gains help to stimulate Britain's early industrialisation? And how far did the Atlantic trading complex provide an impetus for economic change in Britain? These seemingly straightforward questions, it will be shown, are not susceptible of easy answers.

The opening chapter provides a context for tackling these questions by outlining the extent of British transatlantic trade and settlement. It emphasises the economic importance of colonies, the deployment of slave labour and the growth of a rapidly increasing Atlantic trading world during an era that witnessed frequent interruptions to shipping lanes through international wars. The protectionist framework of trade is discussed, with particular reference to the Navigation Acts. The role played by Hanoverian governments in collecting monies to pursue aggressive military and trading policies is also highlighted. The chapter shows that Atlantic trade grew more complex, specialised and interdependent between 1660 and 1800, with close connections forged between merchants and correspondents in far-flung ports. An important role for invisibles in trade occurred, as well as a more obvious rise in the volume and value of imports and exports associated with transatlantic commerce.

Chapter 2 introduces the main debates that have arisen from looking at the economic connections between the New World and Britain in the period when the formal links were at their height. Various debates by economic historians over the respective roles of home and foreign demand at the onset of British industrialisation provide a broad parameter for discussion. These raise problems about the timing and extent of the influence of the growing domestic market and the burgeoning aggregate demand from abroad in stimulating British economic development in the final thirty years of the eighteenth century. The chapter also focuses on the issues stirred up by Eric Williams's *Capitalism and Slavery*, much derided in some quarters but still a seminal influence on the shaping of the problems to be resolved. Williams was the first modern historian to analyse the potential connections between the Caribbean slave–sugar nexus and metropolitan economic development, and the interesting hypotheses he raised still resonate in historical discourse.

Chapter 3 considers evidence on the scale of profits in the African slave trade and whether they were large enough to make a significant impact on national income and industrial investment in Britain. Evidence is produced to show that calculating the profits of transatlantic slaving is a complex issue, subject to varied results, but that the consensus among historians is that such profits were not, in terms of their annual rate of return, the bonanza that was once asserted but, on the contrary, were more modest in scope, though sufficiently good to reflect the opportunity costs offered by the trade. Different handling of data on the ratio of slave trade profits to national income is presented, with disputes among economic historians over the significance of these findings. The chapter concludes with a critique of the methodology of the 'small ratios' approach to economic development – that is, analysing the share of national income provided by a sector or subsector of the economy – by emphasising the limited conclusions such an approach can provide on the dynamic performance of oceanic trade.

This line of analysis is continued in chapter 4, which examines the wealth generated by slavery, the plantation colonies and the wider Atlantic trading complex in relation to Britain's capital accumulation. The sheer wealth of the British Caribbean on the eve of the American Revolution is demonstrated, and consideration given to the debates over the economic well-being of the British West Indian islands in the later eighteenth century. The difficulty of estimating the costs and benefits of empire in relation to the British Caribbean are emphasised and the seemingly limited role of West Indian fortunes in British industrial investment is highlighted. Though capital amassed from the colonies filtered into the industrial sectors of British ports, it has proven difficult to establish that it was decisive for domestic industrial growth. Nor did foreign capital generally play a significant role in early British industrialisation; in fact, Britain had significant foreign debts just before the American Revolution.

Chapter 5 analyses the relationship of exports to transatlantic areas to British economic development, and emphasises the difficulties in gauging whether exports were a spark for growth. The escalating rise of British manufactured exports was very much geared towards American markets over the course of the eighteenth century as demographic growth, increased incomes of white people and consumer demand helped to broaden and increase the volume and value of wares dispatched across the Atlantic. Caribbean-based demand, in particular, helped to boost British exports significantly in the mid-eighteenth century. Though some historians question the importance of exports in stimulating British economic development, a case is presented here for the significant contribution of exports to the national economy – especially those sent across the Atlantic – in terms of the rising share of industrial goods sent abroad, the impact of exports on manufacturing and the significance of exports for industrial employment and the diffusion of new technology in textiles.

Chapter 6 discusses the way in which business and financial institutions were stimulated by slavery and transoceanic trade and the benefits that accrued to Britain as a result. Improvements to the finance of commerce are outlined, including the extensive use of credit via bills of exchange, the growth of banking in British ports after 1750 and the emergence of marine and fire insurance. The changing business strategies pursued in large-scale, complex branches of Atlantic trade and the growth of concentration ratios among merchant firms are discussed to show how business expertise was consolidated and market power extended. The growth in the circulation of business news is outlined to indicate the way in which more accurate judgements about the price and quality of goods and the timing of shipping movements progressed during the eighteenth century. Chapter 7 focuses on the links between Atlantic commercial activity and the growth of British ports, with particular reference to London and the main west coast outports. Data are presented to show the significance of Atlantic trading activity for London, Liverpool, Bristol and Glasgow, and explanations offered as to why they benefited particularly from the growth of transatlantic commerce rather than other British ports. The book aims to cover a wide remit, pulling together disparate evidence and debates. It attempts to marry quantitative and qualitative material; it discusses relevant aspects of economic theory pertaining to the topics examined; it highlights some of the problems of source material for historians working in this field; and it tries to convey the vigour and interest of the ongoing debates on some important exogenous influences on Britain's early industrialisation. Limitations on space and the need to range broadly over the economic affairs of several continents necessitates a succinct exposition of themes. None the less, I have tried to incorporate the most important views from a wide range of historical palettes. Where matters are still unresolved by the state of current research, I have said so; but possibly this book will point towards areas where fruitful new research could be undertaken.

1
The context

The starting point for examining connections between slavery, Atlantic trade and the British economy in the period 1660–1800 lies in the broad reasons for colonial settlement by the English in the seventeenth century and the emergence of slavery as the principal form of large-scale labour organisation in the Atlantic colonies. English curiosity about the New World stimulated voyages of exploration in the sixteenth century. Defeat of the Spanish Armada in 1588 paved the way for English colonisation of the Americas by destroying Spanish naval dominance. English merchants benefiting from the price rises of the sixteenth century formed joint-stock trading companies in the hope of tapping wealth from overseas, notably from the Atlantic world. A greater degree of social and geographical mobility in England, lack of good economic opportunities at home, the lure of new territories as a magnet and serious religious divisions, mainly within Protestantism, provided motives for English people to migrate to colonies in the Stuart era. Settlers from the mother country went to North America and the Caribbean in their thousands as colonisation underwent decades of experimentation. By the end of the seventeenth century around 350,000 English people had crossed the Atlantic.

Before the English Civil War, the main English colonial settlements were in Barbados, the Leeward Islands of Antigua, Nevis and St Christopher, Virginia, Maryland and Massachusetts Bay. In 1655 Cromwell's expeditionary force captured Jamaica from Spain. After the restoration of the Stuart monarchy, new proprietary colonies were established in Carolina, East and West Jersey and Pennsylvania. Colonies also thrived in New England (Rhode Island, New Hampshire, Connecticut, Maine) and Newfoundland. A smattering of territories were permanently added to Britain's Atlantic empire in the eighteenth century. On the North American mainland Georgia was chartered in 1732 under trustees who wished to establish a haven for debtors from British prisons and for Protestant refugees from continental Europe. In the Caribbean four islands – Grenada, Dominica, St Lucia and Tobago – were ceded by the British at the peace treaty that concluded the Seven Years War. By 1776 Britain's Atlantic empire comprised thirteen colonies in North America, the Canadian maritime provinces of Newfoundland, Quebec, Labrador and Nova Scotia, the Hudson's Bay territory and a cluster of Caribbean islands (see maps 1 and 2). There was, of course, also substantial English trade with Asia via the East India Company followed by territorial expansion in India, mainly in Bengal, and English voyages to the Pacific, leading to the white settlement of Australia in 1788; but these are not the focus of the present study.

Already by the mid-seventeenth century the colonies were regarded as markets for manufactured goods and sources of raw materials for the mother country; they absorbed labour and capital and were a source of profits for Britain. By exploiting available land to produce staple commodities, investors in the colonies sought to make good returns. To do so, they needed to organise agricultural plantations to maximise output: this was the most efficient way of achieving gains from abundant land in the Americas. But a large labour force was needed to work on plantations. Attempting to get Native Americans to carry out the work largely failed: the Indians proved poor workers and either resisted such regimes or died out before 1650 through contact with diseases imported from across the ocean. White workers, mainly in the form of indentured servants, could also form the labour force for plantations. However, they became independent at the end of their usual term of service (typically four, five or seven years); they had legal rights that enabled them to negotiate their contractual position in local courts; and their supply dwindled in the late seventeenth century, when the English population underwent a static period and economic conditions improved at home. The next alternative labour supply proved the solution to planters' needs. English merchants followed the Spanish, Portuguese, Dutch and French in shipping large numbers of enslaved Africans across the Atlantic, and put them to work as a captive labour force on plantations. Though it was not essential to

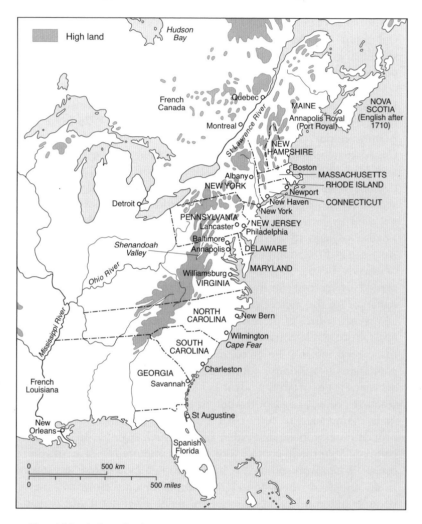

Map 1 North America in 1750

have slaves to cultivate staple crops, African captives working on plantations constituted the workforce that sustained colonial trade with large parts of Europe in the early modern period. Indeed, it could be argued that enduring and firm trade links between Europe and the Americas were not forged until slavery was introduced in the New World.

The Royal African Company, based in London, was the first large-scale English organisation in the slave trade. A successor to the Company of Royal Adventurers, it flourished from 1672 until 1698, when its monopoly charter was rescinded and the slave trade was thrown open to private merchants (Davies, 1957). Thereafter the traffic was dominated by the ports of London, Bristol and, especially, Liverpool. Most slaves were delivered to British colonies in the Americas, but at the Treaty of Utrecht that concluded the War of the Spanish Succession Britain gained the right under the *Asiento* to supply slaves and send an annual merchant ship to Spanish America. This contract continued from 1713 until Walpole's government went to war with Spain in 1739 (Palmer, 1981). The traffic in slaves operated as the famous 'triangular trade'. Textiles, beads, firearms and metalware were shipped to west Africa and bartered or sold for Africans drawn from various tribes in the interior; the slaves were packed tight into the holds of ships for the Atlantic crossing ('the middle passage') and sold in the Americas; and then staple commodities were laden aboard ship for the voyage home and the prospects of sale in the ships' port of origin. The trade and shipping routes followed on each leg of the trade were complex, but the triangular model has proved helpful as a short-hand way of representing the commerce on diagrams and maps (Higman, 1999: 188–92). The slave trade was a grim, exploitative traffic in human beings in which exposure to disease and the possibility of mortality were ever present. Each stage of the voyage involved intricate patterns of supply and demand, which shifted over time. Local and Atlantic-wide factors affected price changes for slaves and determined the number of captives supplied in west Africa and the type and prices of goods sent to procure them. In general, African conditions rather than American demand influenced the ethnicity, age and sex of blacks in the Atlantic slave trade. Once sold in the Americas, most slaves were delivered to plantations to undertake agricultural work based on either the gang or the task system (Anstey, 1975a; Rawley, 1981; Klein, 1990, 1999; Eltis, 2000).

Slave plantations began to flourish in the British Empire in the mid-seventeenth century. During the ensuing century they grew considerably in size, number and significance. By 1750 the black population of the British Empire totalled around 555,000, with some 295,000 living in the Caribbean and 247,000 in North America (P. D. Morgan, 1998: 468). In mainland North America, slaves worked principally on tobacco plantations in Virginia and Maryland (the Chesapeake region) and on rice and indigo plantations in South Carolina and Georgia (the Lower South). They were also found in smaller numbers, not always on plantations, in North Carolina, East Florida, the Mississippi Valley, the middle colonies of Pennsylvania, New Jersey and New York, and New England (notably in Rhode Island). Slaves dominated the labour force of sugar, coffee and cocoa plantations throughout the West Indies, both in the largest British island, Jamaica, and in a series of British possessions in the Windward and Leeward Islands of the eastern Caribbean.

Slave estates needed plenty of land and capital for planting staple crops, and for various buildings, including cooling and drying houses, water mills, distilleries, refineries and slave quarters. Plantations could contain between 50 and 350 slaves, with sugar estates requiring a larger labour force than those catering for other staple crops. The system of chattel slavery, based on racial discrimination and severe legal codes, meant that the offspring of slaves were themselves born into slavery (Curtin, 1990; Walvin, 1993). Because of a high death rate on many plantations, through a combination of hard work, disease and poor diet, the supply of slaves, especially to the West Indies, needed regular replenishment. The eighteenth century was the period when British slave trading was at its peak; some 3 million slaves were carried in British vessels to the Americas during that century, more than by any other European power (D. Richardson, 1989b: 157–8). This formed part of the largest intercontinental forced migration of people in the early modern world, leaving in its wake profound social and cultural changes in the lives of black people. The British did not abolish their slave trade until 1807 and emancipated slaves in their empire (including a relatively small number outside the Caribbean, in Mauritius and the Cape Colony) only in 1834. After a short period of apprenticeship, blacks became fully free in British territories from 1 August 1838.

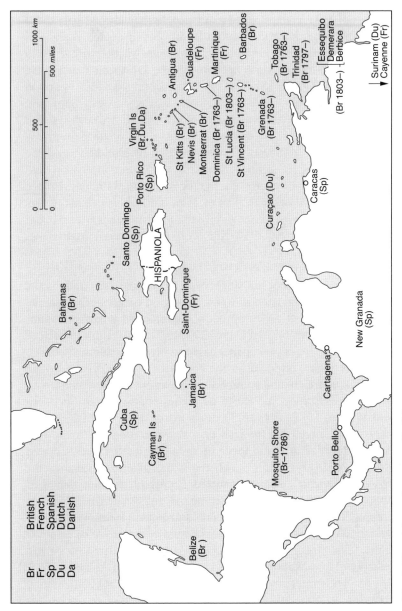

Map 2 The eighteenth-century Caribbean

Br   British
Fr   French
Sp   Spanish
Du   Dutch
Da   Danish

1000 km

500 miles

500

Bahamas (Br)

Santo Domingo (Sp)

HISPANIOLA

Saint-Domingue (Fr)

Cuba (Sp)

Cayman Is (Br)

Jamaica (Br)

Belize (Br)

Mosquito Shore (Br–1786)

Porto Bello

Cartagena

New Granada (Sp)

Caracas (Sp)

Curaçao (Du)

Porto Rico (Sp)

Virgin Is (Br, Du, Da)

St Kitts (Br)

Nevis (Br)

Montserrat (Br)

Dominica (Br 1763–)

St Lucia (Br 1803–)

St Vincent (Br 1763–)

Antigua (Br)

Guadeloupe (Fr)

Martinique (Fr)

Barbados (Br)

Grenada (Br 1763–)

Tobago (Br 1763–)

Trinidad (Br 1797–)

Essequibo (Du)
Demerara
Berbice
(Br 1803–)

Surinam (Du)
Cayenne (Fr)

The transatlantic economy

The plantations and other British possessions in the New World were supplied by ships, goods and people that formed part of an ever-expanding, integrated transatlantic economy. Geographically, this trading complex embraced 2,000 miles of the west African coast, a free trading zone open to all the European powers; the Atlantic wine islands (Madeira, the Azores, the Canaries); ports in continental Europe such as Lisbon, Malaga, Amsterdam and Hamburg; the thirteen mainland North American colonies that became the United States plus Florida; the Canadian maritime provinces; the Caribbean islands, the Bay of Honduras and the Mosquito Shore in central America; and ports in Britain and Ireland. Vessels criss-crossed the ocean from London, Bristol, Liverpool and Glasgow to Boston, New York, Philadelphia, Charleston and Kingston, to name only the most prominent ports, and slaving vessels ranged down the west African coast from Senegambia to Angola.

Some trades operated on a bilateral basis, with vessels shuttling to and fro between ports; but since much British overseas trade in the age of sail was dominated either by full export cargoes or substantial import cargoes but rarely by both, a number of important multilateral trades grew up (see below, 22–3). Because of this imbalance in commodity flows, merchants based in New England or Pennsylvania and New York paid for the goods they received from Britain by shipping, freight and commodity earnings in the provision trades to southern Europe and the West Indies (Pares, 1956; Shepherd and Walton, 1972: 114–36; D. Richardson, 1991). By this means, they compensated for the lack of a staple commodity to provide regular direct returns and made up much of their trade deficit with Britain. In 1768–72, for which fairly full data are available, the North American colonists incurred a current account deficit of about £40,000 per annum, compensating for their deficit in commodity trade with Great Britain and Ireland by earning significant credits in the sale of ships to the mother country plus commissions, insurance, freighting goods and shipment of specie (Shepherd and Walton, 1972: 115; McCusker and Menard, 1985: 80–6). Thus multilateral links 'enabled a system of compensating balances to function long before the better-known settlements

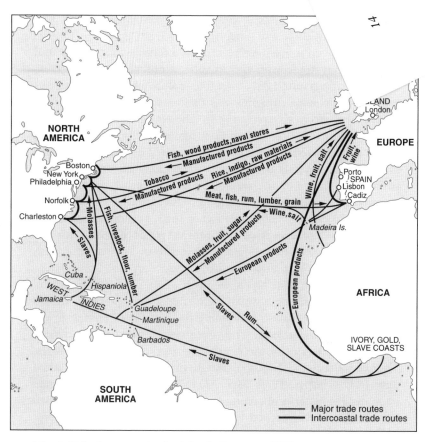

Map 3 Shipping routes in the Atlantic Ocean, c. 1750

pattern of the nineteenth century came into being' (Cain and Hopkins, 1993: 88).

Overseas trade operated under the framework of five Navigation Acts, passed between 1651 and 1696. These provided a large protected market for British manufactures within the empire by confining oceanic trade with the mother country mainly to British-owned and British-manned vessels and by prohibiting the manufacture of various products in the colonies. All colonial and European commodities were to be shipped to Britain or a British colony. An exception was made for certain enumerated commodities, including rice, tobacco, sugar, indigo and naval stores, which could be exported outside the British Empire after first being landed at a British port (Walton and Shepherd, 1979: 66–8, 157). Though Ireland appeared in customs records as a foreign country, most of its commodity trade with the Atlantic world was also subject to these regulations until 1731, when the prohibition on direct imports from British colonial America was removed (except in the case of sugar and tobacco) (Truxes, 1988). The Navigation Laws encouraged Britain to become an entrepôt for importing colonial staples and thus stimulated various re-export trades. They were intended to boost British shipping activity and the number of seamen to give strength to the navy in wartime. This system of protectionism involved placing tariffs on foreign-produced wares and elaborate customs procedures. The Staple Act of 1663, in addition, stipulated that, with a few exceptions, European goods destined for the English Atlantic colonies should be placed aboard ship at an English or Welsh port for shipment across the ocean.

The Navigation Acts lay at the heart of an 'old colonial system' based on mercantilism in which the wealth and sea power of Britain were intended to grow by confining the benefits of empire to the state and its own subjects. They were viewed as a buttress against the economic rivalry of the continental European trading powers. Though subject to various revisions, the Navigation Laws lasted until 1849 (Harper, 1939; McCusker, 1996). They allowed much more flexible patterns of commerce, notably multilateral trade, than the strict controls imposed by Spain on its American dominions, whereby Atlantic shipping was mainly undertaken in bilateral fleets between one Spanish port and a few entrepôts in the Caribbean and South America (McFarlane, 1994: 240). Nevertheless, by the late eighteenth century some leading economic commentators, notably Adam Smith and Josiah Tucker, considered that the Navigation Acts proved a burden to Britain's economic development and that they should be overturned in favour of free trade. But the protectionist system served Hanoverian Britain well, and free trade, despite the advocacy of some high-profile commentators, flourished only some time after Queen Victoria came to the throne. From time to time some historians have argued that enumerated commodities imposed economic costs on the colonies, but the current consensus is that the burdens of the Navigation Acts for the North American colonies was small (Thomas, 1968; Engerman, 1994: 199–200).

Merchants established important commercial connections throughout Britain's Atlantic empire. They travelled between ports or sent captains, agents or supercargoes overseas to conduct business. West India merchants frequently served apprenticeships in the Caribbean, and some were involved in partnerships with personnel based in both Britain and the Caribbean (Devine, 1978; K. Morgan, 1993b). Scottish factors opened stores in the Chesapeake, especially in piedmont areas, where they sold an array of imported goods and dealt with tobacco customers. Some London firms had social and mercantile connections throughout the Atlantic trading world (Price, 1973, vol. I; 1992; Devine, 1975: 55–9, 66–7). Overseas ports had contingents of British merchants. For instance, Lisbon had a community of English merchants and Philadelphia attracted English and Irish businessmen who were socially mobile and searching for economic opportunity (Fisher, 1981; Doerflinger, 1986: 55, 160–1, 335; Truxes, 1988: 118–22). Hanoverian London was home to an international community of merchants and became the leading world centre of finance and trade, a position wrested from Amsterdam in the early eighteenth century (Chapman, 1992: 30). Some London merchants with origins in Scotland, Ireland and the English provinces flourished in Atlantic trade in the mid-eighteenth century, building up interlocking business activities in government funds, military contracting, the slave trade, shipping and landownership in North America, the Caribbean and Britain (Hancock, 1995).

These and other merchant groups established intricate business relations with colonial counterparts, basing their connections on reputation, honour, credit-worthiness and sometimes kinship ties. Risk and uncertainty were central parts of economic enterprise throughout the early modern trading world. Small wonder, then, that personal attributes of probity and trust were essential for consolidating business links in a commercial world in which factors in transatlantic areas were often better placed to make entrepreneurial decisions than their principals (Zahedieh, 1998a; Mathias, 2000). In all these commercial and shipping connections, slavery and the slave trade were central to transatlantic enterprise and to making the British a greater oceanic trading nation than its principal maritime rivals, the French and the Dutch. In *The African Trade, the Great Pillar and Support of the British Plantation Trade* (1745), the mercantilist writer Malachy Postlethwayt summed up this situation by referring to the British Empire as 'a magnificent superstructure of American commerce and naval power on an African foundation' (quoted in E. Williams, 1944: 52).

As this quotation implies, the great circle of commercial exchange was supported with protection on the high seas afforded by the Royal Navy and privateering vessels in the many war years between 1660 and 1800. Britain was at war for 55 of 140 years in that period. These wars had a significant colonial component. Moreover, Britain achieved naval hegemony over the French, its chief colonial rivals, over this period. The War of the League of Augsburg (1689–97) and the War of the Spanish Succession (1702–13) both partially involved conflict between the French and the English in the Atlantic (Jones, 1988). The War of Jenkins's Ear (1739–42) was rooted in rivalries with Spain in the Caribbean. The War of the Austrian Succession (1742–8) partly involved a power struggle with the French in the same theatre of conflict. The Seven Years War (1756–63) witnessed the triumph of British hegemony over France in North America (Pares, 1936). The first British Empire began to crumble, however, with the loss of the American colonies in the War of Independence (1776–83), a conflict that also witnessed struggles between European maritime rivals in the West Indies. The first years of the wars against revolutionary France (1793–1801) saw renewed Anglo-French conflict in that theatre, exacerbated by the huge slave rebellion in Saint-Domingue (Duffy, 1987).

Thus Britain's consolidation of a marine empire overseas involved considerable struggle and international rivalry. Trade was often interrupted; freight and insurance rates increased; and convoy protection was needed for commerce with the Caribbean. British privateers based in London, Liverpool, Bristol and the Channel Islands helped to stem the tide of depredations by foreign shipping (Crowhurst, 1977; Starkey, 1990). More important, the navy over-came most of the challenges it faced from war on the high seas. Britain maintained a wartime fleet of between 185 and 350 vessels in the first half of the eighteenth century, partly augmented by a construction programme and partly by capturing good-quality enemy shipping. By this means, it could establish supremacy over the combined fleets of France and Spain. Thus in the wars between

1739 and 1763 the British, despite danger and alarms, preserved their sugar colonies from invasion and economic catastrophe; the French suffered far more in these wars than the British (Pares, 1936: 471).

The navy enforced the Navigation Acts and gradually secured command of the English Channel against French and Spanish rivalry; by consolidating British security vis-à-vis their main European maritime rivals, command of the world was feasible (Harding, 1995: 114–43; Rodger, 1998).

In addition, the taxes collected by the British fiscal-military state to back military power were substantial; without them the economic benefits accruing to Britain from the colonies would have been seriously impaired. Taxes collected rose by a multiplier of 14.4 in the period 1688–1815 and successive governments borrowed extensively to fund the national debt. In wartime British governments could borrow large sums of money at several percentage points lower than those the king of France could achieve. Large tranches of these monies served to bolster naval and military forces. They enabled the state to support overseas trading activity on a substantial scale. By these means, the eighteenth-century British people became second only to the Dutch as the most heavily taxed subjects in Europe (Brewer, 1989; O'Brien, 1998: 63–70). The bureaucracy of the British state grew and became more efficient with the development of government offices such as the Admiralty, Customs, Excise, the Board of Trade, the Treasury Board, the Victualling Board and the Colonial Office. British sinews of power in the eighteenth century were thus heavily centred on naval, financial and bureaucratic resources. Whether these resources underpinned a 'blue-water' defence policy directed towards long-term imperial ends or, on the contrary, were primarily intended to secure the realm against foreign depredations is still debated by historians (Baugh, 1994: 189–90; Rodger, 1998: 170). Nevertheless, the aggressive military and foreign policies of Hanoverian governments helped to secure the long-term progress of the British economy, and played a significant part in facilitating British dominance of international trade and financial services by the time of the Napoleonic wars (O'Brien, 1994).

The growth of overseas trade

Statistics on trade indicate the growing contribution of overseas commerce to Britain's economic vitality. The main trends are summarised in table 1.

These are official figures based on the fixed valuations given to individual commodities by the Inspector General of Imports and Exports at the beginning of the eighteenth century; they therefore are not an index to the current value of trade. Nevertheless, they provide a good proxy for the growing volume of commerce. Regular trade returns were not collected by the state before 1696, though scattered statistics on the volume and value of trade survive, notably for London (Davis, 1954; Zahedieh, 1998b). Thereafter the Inspector General's customs returns provide a firm basis for examining the quantitative dimensions of overseas trade. English domestic exports and retained imports both quadrupled over the course of the eighteenth century: English domestic exports were worth nearly £4.5 million in 1700–1 and British domestic exports reached a level of £18.2 million in 1797–8. English retained imports grew from £5.8 million to £23.9 million between the same two sets of years. This growth was accompanied by a marked shift in the pattern of trade: the transatlantic sector expanded while trade with Europe experienced relative decline. In 1700–1, the colonies in the New World accounted for 11 per cent of the value of English exports and for 20 per cent of imports. In other words, Europe still dominated British overseas trade at the start of the eighteenth century. This pattern changed, however, over subsequent decades. By 1772–3, North America and the West Indies took 38 per cent of exports and provided 39 per cent of imports. By 1797–8, North America and the West Indies received 57 per cent of British exports and supplied 32 per cent of imports.

Re-exports grew fivefold from £2,136,000 in 1700–1 to £11,802,000 in 1797–8. They were mainly supplied to European ports and included many colonial commodities such as tobacco, sugar, rice and coffee (Davis, 1962–3; 1979: 102–3; Deane and Cole, 1967: 87; Ormrod, 1984). The re-export trade, encouraged by Parliament's permission to draw back many import duties, enabled Britain to maintain trade with ports in northern Europe with which little commerce would have otherwise been conducted.

Table 1 *Geographical distribution of British overseas trade, 1700–98 (per cent distributions)*

	1700–1 England	1730–1 England	1750–1 England	1772–3 Britain	1797–8 Britain
Retained imports from:					
Ireland	5	4	9	11	13
Europe	62	52	46	34	29
North America	6	9	11	15	7
West Indies	14	21	19	24	25
Africa	1	1	1	1	1
East Indies and other	12	13	14	15	25
Total	100	100	100	100	100
	(£5,819,000)	(£7,386,000)	(£7,855,000)	(£13,395,000)	(£23,903,000)
Domestic exports to:					
Ireland	3	5	8	10	9
Europe	82	76	69	39	21
North America	6	7	11	26	32
West Indies	5	7	5	12	25
Africa	2	2	1	5	4
East Indies and other	2	3	6	8	9
Total	100	100	100	100	100
	(£4,461,000)	(£5,203,000)	(£9,125,000)	(£10,196,000)	(£18,298,000)

Table 1 *(Cont.)*

	1700–1 England	1730–1 England	1750–1 England	1772–3 Britain	1797–8 Britain
Re-exports:					
Ireland	7	11	18	18	11
Europe	78	70	62	65	78
North America	5	7	11	9	3
West Indies	6	6	4	3	4
Africa	3	4	3	4	3
East Indies and other	1	2	2	1	1
Total	100 (£2,136,000)	100 (£3,002,000)	100 (£3,428,000)	100 (£6,930,000)	100 (£11,802,000)

Source: Deane and Cole (1967): 87. The valuations given here are in 'official' rather than current prices.

It therefore fitted the interdependent pattern of Atlantic trading activity already discussed. As Jacob M. Price has noted, re-exports 'helped pay for the imports of all those useful raw materials from northern Europe – especially iron, flax, hemp, masts, deals, pitch, and tar – that kept thousands of sailors and tens of thousands of workers busy in Britain' (Price, 1998: 86).

British exports sent across the Atlantic were mainly finished manufactured wares such as textiles, hardware, metalware and glassware. Imports from the Americas were dominated by sugar, tobacco, rice, coffee, raw cotton, wheat, naval stores, dyestuffs and other products increasingly in demand with British and European consumers. The most lucrative of these products were staple commodities grown in the tropical or semi-tropical colonies rather than in temperate zones, exotic fruits that gradually but inexorably became important components of the British diet (Walvin, 1997). During the eighteenth century, British foreign trade changed from being largely an exchange of woollens for raw materials to being based on a wider range of manufactured exports exchanged for foodstuffs. Refined sugar became a significant part of the British diet in the eighteenth century; per capita consumption increased from 1 lb to 25 lb between 1670 and 1770, with many ordinary folk, as well as wealthier consumers, acquiring a sweet tooth. Tobacco in the form of snuff or cut or roll tobacco, smoked in clay pipes, reached a domestic market in which demand was limited and inelastic; but tobacco was an important re-exported commodity to France, the Netherlands and Germany (Price, 1973, 1984; Shammas, 1990: 78–83). Rice was another significant re-exported staple that usually had a small market in Britain, because home-grown foodstuffs plus high import duties on rice deterred its mass consumption (Coclanis, 1989; Nash, 1992).

Invisible aspects of trade unrepresented in the customs figures expanded the scope of British overseas trading activity; they augmented the revenues from the export of British commodities overseas and covered up some of the deficits on the balance of commodity trade (O'Brien, 1998: 54–5). In 1740 Robert Dinwiddie estimated that the amount of cash, dyes, drugs, cocoa and other commodities imported to the British plantations through trade with the Spanish and French possessions in the Americas amounted to £425,000 annually. Prize goods, mainly from the Caribbean, had an annual average value of £438,794 in the Seven Years War. In 1691 Jamaica's bullion exports were worth £100,000. Some £2,368,484 worth of bullion alone was sent to England from the West Indies in the period 1748–65 (Sheridan, 1973: 318–19, 426–7, 451–2). The increasingly interdependent nature of seaborne commerce meant that large imports of hemp, flax, timber and naval stores from the Baltic region were partly fuelled by the growth of demand for shipbuilding materials for vessels plying Atlantic shipping routes (Farnie, 1962–3: 213).

Other invisible trades included triangular ventures such as the slave trade between west Africa, North America/the British Caribbean and Britain; the Newfoundland cod trade, in which the sales of fish were concentrated in the Iberian peninsula; the trade in wine from Madeira and the Azores to an array of ports throughout the Atlantic trading basin; and the trades in linen and provisions from Ireland to Newfoundland and the West Indies. The provisions sent from Ireland consisted of beef, butter, pork and herrings, and the trade was not subject to legislative interference (Fisher, 1971: 71–6; Anstey, 1975a; Nash, 1985; Truxes, 1988: 147–92; Hancock, 2000). Leaving aside the slave trade (considered fully below, 36–48) recent estimates have suggested that the earnings for English merchants and shippers in the three other multilateral trades amounted to £661,000 in 1700 and £1,314,000 in 1770 (Nash, 1997: 122–3). Britain also benefited from significant levels of trade in goods and slaves with Spanish America and Brazil. A contemporary calculated that the entrepôt trade between Britain and the Spanish West Indies, concerned with slaves and contraband, comprised nearly £300,000 per year between 1670 and 1702 (Sheridan, 1965: 18). 'Informal empire' trade led to a minimum of £40 million of Brazilian gold and Spanish American silver flowing back to Britain between 1700 and 1750, suggesting that imports of these precious metals were on a par with the importation of sugar and tobacco from the 'formal empire' in the same period (Crouzet, 1990; Richardson and Evans, 1996). H. E. S. Fisher has suggested to me that some 60 per cent of the expansion of English exports to Portugal over the first sixty years of the eighteenth century was due to re-exports to Brazil and the stimulus to Portuguese metropolitan demand derived from Brazilian prosperity. In addition, the increase in English manufactured exports to Spain between 1700 and 1750

comprised about one-eighth of the total increase of English manufactured exports, and many of these wares were re-exported to
Spanish America (Fisher, 1971: 1–9, 16). Clearly, multilateral and
invisible trades were more important in the eighteenth-century
British Empire than is usually realised (Baugh, 1994: 196–9).

The smuggling of tobacco, wine and brandy into Britain was also
significant in the eighteenth century because of high import tariffs.
Smuggled tobacco imported from Virginia and Maryland, obviously
not counted for customs purposes, probably accounted for about
one-third of British tobacco consumption by 1750 (Nash, 1982:
372). There were even more complex trades such as those carried
out by vessels taking rice from South Carolina and Georgia for
quick re-export, after entering British customs, to markets in the
Netherlands and Germany and then sailing back to their home port
laden with produce and raw materials from Europe (timber and bar
iron from the Baltic ports, for example). Shipping and insurance
services must be included among the invisible aspects of foreign
commerce (see below, 76). Interdependency in trade also affected
the slave trade. The largest single item in the export trade to Africa
consisted of East Indian textiles; they comprised 40 per cent of
textiles and 27 per cent of all goods shipped from England to Africa
between 1699 and 1800 (Klein, 1990: 292). Other commodities
prominent among re-exports to Africa in the slave trade were
Swedish bar iron, Italian beads and German linens ('osnaburghs')
(D. Richardson, 1985: 5).

The sheer scope of the changes in British foreign trade in the
century after 1660 was striking when compared with what came
before. Whereas overseas commerce had been concentrated for
centuries on shipping with European ports and with a limited range
and value of exports and imports, oceanic trade in the century after
the restoration of the Stuart monarchy extended its geographical
scope across the globe and augmented the types of goods found in
ships' cargoes as well as their value. Important trades that were to
some extent invisible in customs records, notably the Atlantic slave
trade, became prominent in connection with British overseas territories in this period. The increasing sophistication and interdepen-
dence of the eighteenth-century Atlantic economy led to greater
levels of capitalisation in foreign trade and more specialised commercial processes, such as the extension of credit ties, the evolution

of complex mercantile practices and the growth in the size and market power of merchant firms (see ch. 6 for a fuller discussion). Ralph Davis referred to these changes in early modern British overseas trade as a 'Commercial Revolution', and suggested cautiously that the 'important changes in industry and in the English economy as a whole, under the influence of developments in overseas trade . . . were undoubtedly essential as a prelude to the greater movement' (i.e. the Industrial Revolution) (Davis, 1967: 23–4). Debates that explicitly link the contribution of slavery and the Atlantic trades to British economic development in the eighteenth century are thus considered in the next chapter.

2

The debates

What were the economic benefits of this expanding transoceanic commercial network to the mother country? The answer to the question is complex, which is why so much ink has been spilt on the matter. As early as the 1770s, the political economist Adam Smith pointed to the colonies as a drain on British resources. He argued that profits arising from them filled the coffers of certain interest groups such as merchants and planters but did not benefit the economy as a whole: this empire was 'a project which has cost, which continues to cost, and which, if pursued in the same way as it has been hitherto, is likely to cost, immense expence, without being likely to bring any profit; for the effects of the monopoly of the colony trade, it has been shewn, are, to the great body of the people, mere loss instead of profit' (quoted in Sheridan, 1973: 5–7). Smith's view was that the gains from foreign trade could have been obtained without the costly administrative and defence costs of empire. On the other hand, the eminent conservative political thinker Edmund Burke regarded the preservation of the empire as of paramount economic importance by pointing to the sheer growth in the proportion of British trade that the colonies accounted for. Noting that the exports from England comprised one-twelfth of English colonial trade in 1700 and one-third in 1775, Burke stated: 'This is the relative proportion of the importance of the colonies at these two periods; and all reasoning concerning our mode of treating them must have this proportion as its basis, or it is a reasoning weak, rotten, and sophistical' (quoted ibid.).

Historians have similarly failed to reach consensus on whether burgeoning international trade stimulated the British economy in the eighteenth century. Some depict foreign trade as an 'engine of growth' that enabled merchants to exploit productivity advances in widening markets abroad, and suggest that rising demand for imports stimulated the expansion of the export industries and overall economic growth (e.g. Berrill, 1960; Deane and Cole, 1967: 83, 86–9; Lee, 1986: 107–24). In one such interpretation, foreign trade was a trigger for a 'take-off' into self-sustained growth in the last two decades of the eighteenth century, providing a quick, sharp boost, with imports generating exports and vice versa (Habakkuk and Deane, 1963: 77–80). According to Eric Hobsbawm, foreign trade was the match that lit the torch of industrialisation: 'home demand increased – but foreign demand multiplied. If a spark was needed, this is where it came from' (Hobsbawm, 1968: 48). A broader emphasis on the importance of colonisation and trade for metropolitan economic development has been put forward by the geographer J. M. Blaut, who has argued that the great demand that Europeans generated in the colonies, 'more than anything else, pushed the Industrial Revolution forward' (Blaut, 1993: 206).

Arguments emphasising the significance of long-distance commerce for the metropolitan economy draw support from the dynamic performance of overseas trade in a British economy that experienced gradual growth for most of the eighteenth century. Despite marked fluctuations in wartime trading, the annual level of trade rose by 0.8 per cent between 1700 and 1740, by 1.7 per cent between 1740 and 1770 and by 2.6 per cent between 1770 and 1800 – a faster rate of growth than that of total output (Deane and Cole, 1967: 46). Thus trade accelerated just around the time in the late eighteenth century that Britain began to industrialise: in other words, in the decades that factories, canals, steam engines, labour productivity, increased manufacturing and a rising wage-earning populace were beginning to transform the structure and pace of economic life. Overseas trade also contributed significantly to national income in the period 1780–1801, when an export boom, largely directed to transatlantic markets, led to a 19.3 per cent increase in the incremental ratio of exports to GNP (Crafts, 1985: 131–2). After 1780 foreign demand for British exports has been seen as contributing powerfully to industrial expansion in Britain (Bairoch, 1973). Certainly, the growth in exports in the final two decades of the eighteenth century was greater than during any previous period in that epoch.

Other historians place more emphasis on the home market as the mainspring of growth, suggesting that domestic demand made a more decisive impact on industrial output than the growth of overseas demand (e.g. Flinn, 1966: 62). Some emphasise the agricultural advance of the period 1660–1800 as the chief stimulus for economic growth (Bairoch, 1973). Others regard the progressive cheapening of food between 1730 and 1750, the rise in middle-range incomes and the changing tastes of a swiftly rising population undergoing a 'consumer revolution' as stimuli for the production of manufactured goods mainly for domestic rather than foreign markets from the 1740s onwards (e.g. John, 1965; Eversley, 1967; McKendrick, Brewer and Plumb, 1983: 1–33). The extent of agricultural progress and the consumer revolution, however, are still much debated. Did an agricultural revolution occur in eighteenth-century Britain? Was the consumer revolution a phenomenon that percolated outwards from London to the provinces? Did it involve social emulation by poorer folk of their social betters? Did it depend on new marketing and commercial skills and the role played by women and children as consumers (Hudson, 1992: 173–80)? These unresolved issues mean that emphasis on the growth of the domestic market as the mainspring for economic development still needs further analysis.

It has been suggested that lack of evidence for variations in British retained imports systematically preceding variations in exports supports an emphasis on the home market as the impetus for growth. In this argument imports after 1745 were regarded as stemming from the export of domestic goods and not vice versa (Hatton, Lyons and Satchell, 1983). The growth of British industry as a result of falling production and transaction costs in the domestic economy has also received firm support. Thus Robert P. Thomas and D. N. McCloskey argued that no single trade was vital to the nation's prosperity in the eighteenth century, that the profits of the slave trade were not fed significantly into British industry, and that the gains from trade were relatively small in relation to the increase in per capita income. They concluded that, 'in the late eighteenth century, the strongest effect between commerce abroad and industry at home was from industrialisation to commerce, not the reverse. Trade was the child of industry' (Thomas and McCloskey, 1981: 102).

Other assessments modified this position but were still reluctant to grant foreign trade a significant exogenous role in Britain's early industrialisation. One historian noted that 'trade . . . grew with the industrial revolution, rather than starting it' (Kindleberger, 1975: 632). Ralph Davis referred to the transformation of economic endeavour wrought by 'a commercial revolution' (see ch. 1), but regarded this as a prelude to industrialisation rather than part of the Industrial Revolution (Davis, 1967: 23–4). Another approach has been to suggest that Britain's industrialisation began because of the multiple economic factors that interacted in the late eighteenth century, including agricultural progress and greater manufacturing, but that foreign trade profits, though they provided some stimulus, were insufficiently large to make a difference 'at the margin' (Bairoch, 1973). These widely divergent views on the links between foreign trade and the economy as a whole are difficult to assess partly because the historians cited tend not, on the whole, to develop their arguments with supporting data; the views quoted are often summary opinions rather than the result of a sustained marshalling of appropriate evidence. The positions taken are also difficult to assess in the absence of convincing indices on the terms of trade in the eighteenth century that would enable us to compare trends in export and import prices (O'Brien and Engerman, 1991: 191).

Economic historians are universally agreed that the expansion of trade and colonisation was integral to British economic development in the eighteenth century, but they have disagreed over the precise interrelationship of the various economic factors involved. This is not surprising given that much of the relevant quantitative data is still in need of refinement and that only a limited number of economic models have been applied to the subject. Moreover, at the level of theory it has proven difficult to offer a counterfactual model of how the British economy would have benefited more if extra resources had been placed directly into the domestic marketplace rather than allocated to external trade, defence costs, trading posts and colonies. Because underemployment, buttressed by a parish-based Poor Law, was a central characteristic of eighteenth-century Britain, it is difficult to offer an alternative model of how Britain would have progressed better economically based on full utilisation of resources at home.

This discussion seeks to clarify matters by outlining the distinctive ways in which colonial trade and the slave labour it sustained were significant for British economic development in the period 1660–1800, especially after 1750. This can serve a useful purpose in integrating the work of historians of the early Industrial Revolution in Britain with the findings of specialists in foreign trade, while drawing on the perspective of Caribbean scholars and historians of slavery. It is timely to do this because over the past thirty years explanations of Britain's early industrialisation have tended to emphasise the arguments in favour of a growing domestic market as the spur for increased manufacturing production (Inikori, 2000). In general, most mainstream British economic historians have not considered the implications of empire and slavery for the onset of industrialisation. Martin Daunton's recent large textbook *Progress and Poverty: An Economic and Social History of Britain 1700–1850* (1995) is a typical example: it includes interesting material on merchants and marketing and on the significance of export demand in the eighteenth century, but does not engage with the literature linking slavery and the slave trade to British industrialisation. As one reviewer of the book put it: 'it is hard for students to reach a balanced assessment of slavery's economic significance when some Caribbean specialists portray it as crucial to British industrialization and economic history textbooks ignore it almost completely' (*Economic History Review*, 49, 1996: 600).

The Williams thesis

The most influential discussion of the connections between slavery, Atlantic trade and the eighteenth-century British economy is Eric Williams's *Capitalism and Slavery* (1944), a revision of an Oxford doctorate in history dating from the late 1930s. Williams, a Caribbean scholar and politician who later in life became the first prime minister of independent Trinidad and Tobago, was convinced of the economic impact of slavery and the colonial trading system on Britain's industrialisation. Writing at a time when Africa and the Caribbean were marginalised by European historians, Williams opposed what one scholar has termed 'the colonizers' model of the world', that is, the notion that economic and social change in a global context was the result of geographical diffusion from Europe to the 'periphery' (Blaut, 1993). Well aware of his West Indian audience as well as of the political implications of his historical work, Williams wrote as an economic determinist influenced by Marxist ideas. Marx, of course, had linked the slave trade to industrial capitalism and had emphasised the connection between the two as a crucial part of the global process that promoted capitalism. This was a viewpoint that Williams absorbed intuitively and intellectually.

Williams publicised the exploitation of his native region by European settlers; but he was also influenced by more traditional issues treated by the imperial historians of his day (such as the growth of humanitarianism and the attitude of European imperial politicians towards colonial subjects). His motivation was both academic and rhetorical. The integration of the Caribbean into a broader economic system based on international capitalism and the centrality of slavery and plantations as the fulcrum of that development were twin focal points of his work (Beckles, 1998). To emphasise these interconnections served both to delineate the historical growth of slave-dominated staple economies in the West Indies and the legacy of poverty and underdevelopment that came after slave emancipation. Williams did not concentrate as much in his writings on racism in relation to slavery, though there are relevant passages in *Capitalism and Slavery* that are quite explicit on this theme. At the beginning of the book, for instance, Williams asserted that 'Slavery was not born of racism: rather, racism was the consequence of slavery' (1944: 7). He preferred to see slavery as 'basically an economic phenomenon' (ibid.), partly because to concentrate on the economics of slavery and the slave trade and their legacy was to tackle the most promising way in which the poverty and plight of black people could be improved.

Williams argued that the slave trade and the sale of sugar in Britain provided a significant amount of the capital and the demand for the growth of British manufactured goods in the later eighteenth century. Emphasising the wealth generated by the slave trade and the sugar–slave nexus of the Caribbean, Williams explicitly regarded these as major components of Britain's transition to an industrial nation. The West India merchants and planters, in his analysis, were the entrepreneurs driving this commerce, who wielded an important influence on economic and political affairs in Britain. Though he did not discount the accumulation of capital and investible funds from Britain's domestic economy in the eighteenth century, he still underscored the significance of the inflow of capital from the West Indies as a crucial stimulus for the structural economic changes that occurred in the early phase of Britain's transition to industrialisation. He also linked his findings to the changing political economy of British involvement in its empire in the late eighteenth century; to the supposed 'swing to the east' in British overseas expansion after the loss of the American colonies; to the economic state of the West Indies; and to the abolition of the British slave trade and slavery (E. Williams, 1944). In pursuing these themes Williams wrote on a geographically wide scale, attempting to explore the interrelated economic development of four continents. Few historians had attempted such an ambitious agenda at the time he wrote. He made it impossible for historians to discuss British economic development in the eighteenth century without consideration of slavery and the slave trade.

Williams argued that the free trade ideas of Adam Smith signalled a shift away from mercantilism and slavery in Britain's imperial economy in the late eighteenth century and that the rise of industrial capitalism and free wage labour were seen as their successors. The turning point in this perceived transition from mercantilism to a new industrial capitalism came with the American War of Independence, when the Caribbean islands were subject to much economic privation (see also Carrington, 1988). In the new post-war British economic order symbolised by manufacturers, machines and factories, the West Indian plantation system had a reduced significance for British capitalists. Williams connected this transition to an argument about the declining economic returns from sugar plantations in the British Caribbean after 1763, pointing to diminishing profits and overproduction on sugar estates. He argued that British perceptions of this decline caused its statesmen to abolish the slave trade because it was no longer viable. In framing his arguments he attacked the prevailing imperial school of British historians he had encountered when studying at Oxford, particularly their emphasis on abolitionism as stemming from the altruistic humanitarian work of William Wilberforce, Thomas Clarkson and other members of the Clapham Sect. Williams later included many of these arguments in more general, synthetic books such as *From Columbus to Castro: The History of the Caribbean 1492–1969* (1970). A critique of the older school of British imperial historians can be found in his book *British Historians and the West Indies* (1964). These later books were not as rigorous as *Capitalism and Slavery* in their use of historical evidence; they used history to promote nation-building in Trinidad, to emphasise the regional importance of the Caribbean and to combat colonialism. They were written long after Williams had forsaken academic life for the world of politics (Higman, 1999: 90–7).

Because Williams wrote pithily but on a grand scale, it is difficult to pin down specific connections between the wide-ranging ideas and evidence he adduced in *Capitalism and Slavery* (Engerman, 1975: 332). And with the passage of time part of his conceptual framework has withered away. Historians today, for instance, do not draw such a sharp distinction between the ending of mercantilism and the growth of free trade and industrial capitalism; indeed some are unhappy with the use of mercantilism as a concept, arguing that British overseas expansion did not conform to a set of planned economic policies. Nor do most historians now consider that a shift in imperial policy towards the east really occurred after the American Revolution. In addition, each of Williams's major assertions has been challenged by subsequent research, as we shall see, and his work has had supporters as well as detractors. Many of the points raised have been frequently summarised, but with no consensus on many issues (e.g. McDonald, 1979; Beckles, 1984; Solow and Engerman, 1987; Minchinton, 1983, 1996).

Some historians have noted that germs of many of Williams's ideas can be found in earlier writers from the Victorian period and in Wilson E. Williams's *Africa and the Rise of Capitalism* (1938), a short work based on a master's thesis written at Howard University, where Eric Williams had an academic appointment in the years he was preparing *Capitalism and Slavery* for publication (e.g. Darity, 1988; Inikori, forthcoming). Wilson Williams argued, for instance, that the African slave trade 'was a very important factor in the growth of the capitalist economy in England' because it furnished a considerable market for English manufactured goods; it provided profits that were eventually 'turned from purely commercial to industrial employment'; and it stimulated the shipbuilding industry.

Moreover, the West Indian plantation economy was also important in the development of English capitalism because some of the large fortunes arising from the exploitation of black slave labour were 'transferred to the mother country, and eventually invested in industrial enterprise'. Wilson Williams's conclusion was that 'without the Negro slave it is likely that neither the African trade nor the West Indian economy could have played an important part in the development of English capitalism; and hence it is unlikely that without the slave trade, English capitalism could have shown the phenomenal growth it did' (all quoted in Bailey, 1986: 23). The phrases quoted are strikingly similar to passages in *Capitalism and Slavery*, as any reader of that book will realise. I have dwelt on them to indicate the way in which Wilson Williams's ideas were soon exploited by Eric Williams.

Others have found that it is not always clear exactly what the Williams thesis was because the main arguments are often referred to allusively in *Capitalism and Slavery*. Still others have demonstrated that the book was, in an important sense, a polemical and political tract asserting West Indian nationalism as much as a contribution to professional history. Along with C. L. R. James's *The Black Jacobins: Toussaint l'Ouverture and the San Domingo Revolution* (1938), it was a pioneer of 'Third World scholarship' of an anti-colonial bent, one of the first extended modern treatments of West Indian history written by a Caribbean scholar that laid the foundations for academic respectability among historians from that region (Beckles, 1984: 172; 1987; Drescher, 1987: 193–4; Menard, 1998: 795). Even in the Caribbean, notably in Trinidad and Tobago, there has been fierce discussion not just about Williams's political legacy but about the merits of his historical ideas. This is as true in the first decade of the twenty-first century as it was thirty years before. The main support for Williams's arguments in *Capitalism and Slavery* has come from black scholars, though not exclusively; the main detractors are white historians (Darity, 1998: 814). This reflects the fact that contributors to the debate over the 'Williams thesis' have often been motivated as much by ethics and ideology as by an attempt to arrive at historical truth. In some instances, scholars seem more interested in finding regular academic outlets for their predisposed views rather than proving their case persuasively.

There is justification for challenging the details of *Capitalism and Slavery*. Williams wrote at a time when statistical presentation in economic history was much less rigorous than today. His discussions of mercantilism were based very much on the tracts of seventeenth- and eighteenth-century writers, and his data were often taken from their compilations. One could argue that this approach to his research gave him empathy for the contemporary mercantilist view of the colonies as a source of wealth for the metropolis (O'Shaughnessy, 2000). Even with the statistics at his disposal, however, Williams ignored material or used partial evidence; for instance, he had very patchy data on sugar and slave prices and failed to produce any convincing estimates of the profitability of Caribbean sugar plantations to substantiate his thesis that overproduction caused the abolition of Britain's slave trade (Anstey, 1968: 315, 318–19). The chinks in his evidential base allowed other historians to challenge him. Seymour Drescher's *Econocide: British Slavery in the Era of Abolition* (1977), in particular, produced a mass of material to argue against Williams's position on the decline of the British Caribbean and the economic reasons for abolition of the slave trade, and his arguments will be examined more closely in chapter 4.

Yet many general ideas contained in *Capitalism and Slavery* have proved to be durable, even if hotly challenged; the general verdict on the book is summed up in one historian's catchy phrase 'down but not out' (Beckles, 1982). The challenge for historians taking up the main themes of Williams's work is 'to explain Britain's *lack of uniqueness* in regard to slavery and the slave trade and its *uniqueness* in regard to economic growth and industrial development' (Engerman, 1995: 168–9). The reason for this is that slavery and the slave trade had very small effects on the industrialisation of other European powers such as Spain, Portugal, France and the Netherlands even though they each had a substantial commitment to empire and slavery (Drescher, 1997). Another broad theme that merits close attention is whether the magnitude of the gains from slavery and Atlantic trade were sufficient in themselves to lift Britain to a leading world economic position by the late eighteenth century (Engerman, 1995: 155).

This book makes frequent reference to those sections in *Capitalism and Slavery* that are directly connected with the economic impact of empire and slavery on Georgian Britain; other parts of the Williams thesis, notably those dealing with abolitionism, are treated in less depth because they are not central to the main thrust of this discussion, which is to interpret the relevant scholarship of the past half-century to examine the precise connections between slavery, Atlantic trade and the British economy in the period from the mid-seventeenth century to the era of Britain's initial industrialisation. Like Williams, I attempt to trace these connections within a global economic setting so that one can link trade, commerce, business, population growth and living standards in North America, the West Indies and Britain, with some attention to developments in west Africa.

3

The profits of the slave trade

The British slave trade flourished mainly from the restoration of the Stuart monarchy until it was abolished by parliamentary act by the 'Ministry of All the Talents'. During that period British slaving vessels dominated the Guinea traffic, delivering around half of all the slaves shipped from Africa to America. The trade escalated over time. Annual shipments of enslaved Africans increased about sixfold in the century after 1660 before levelling out or declining (D. Richardson, 1998: 441). The immorality of trading in human cargoes was widely recognised only after 1770, with the growth of an abolitionist movement based on Enlightenment values of rationality and progress in human endeavour, as part of which slavery and the slave trade appeared to be peculiarly retrogressive institutions. The spread of Christian benevolence, the belief in God's providence in a fallen world and the notion of progressive revelation in the second half of the eighteenth century also helped to promote an anti-slavery viewpoint (Anstey, 1975a: 91–235). The Quakers, Anglican evangelicals and Methodists who were prominent in the early anti-slave trade movement, as well as other enlightened observers, condemned the greed of slave merchants. For instance, the Revd Richard Watson, a prominent Methodist preacher, referred to Bristol as 'a dark den of slave traders'; and a visitor to George Washington's Mount Vernon noted that slavery was allowed to flourish in North America because of 'the greed of the Liverpool merchants who before the [American] Revolution peopled this Country with Blacks' (K. Morgan, 1993a: 128; Budka, 1965: 105).

Implicit in these attacks was the notion that the slave trade represented an unpleasant scramble to get rich while black Africans suffered. The profits gained via the slave trade could be made in various ways. As well as direct gains from slave sales, there was money acquired from speculation on commodities shipped on triangular voyages, from the circulation of money, from credit extension and from other forms of risk capital (Robinson, 1987: 134). The financial rewards accruing from such commerce appeared to be staggering. Thus evidence from Bristol and Liverpool points to a trade that attracted substantial investment and generated great gains. Bristol merchants invested £50,000–60,000 annually in the slave trade c. 1710–11, over £150,000 per annum in the 1730s and £280,100 on average in the period 1788–92 (D. Richardson, 1986: xvii; 1996: xviii). The annual sums invested in Liverpool's slave trade were c. £200,000 in 1750 and probably more than £1 million in 1800 (D. Richardson, 1994: 75). Individual merchants could reap a considerable amount of booty from trafficking in slaves. Henry Bright and Richard Meyler sen., who traded from Bristol in the slave and West India trades, left fortunes of £50,000 and £30,000 respectively (K. Morgan, 1993a: 186). John Tarleton, a Liverpudlian slave merchant, saw his wealth grow from £6,000 in 1748 to almost £80,000 in 1773. Thomas Leyland, another Liverpool slave trader who became a banker, had a fortune worth over £736,000 just before he died in 1827 (D. Richardson, 1994: 76).

These impressive fortunes tell us little directly, however, about the profitability of the slave trade and its economic contribution to Britain. Providing convincing evidence on this matter has not proven easy because, from the late eighteenth century onwards, estimates of the profits generated in the British slave trade have been subject to considerable disagreement. In 1750 Malachy Postlethwayt considered that Britain's annual gain from participation in the slave trade amounted to £1,648,600 (Darity, 1992a: 272). In the late 1780s contemporaries giving evidence to parliamentary committees set up to examine the conduct of the slave trade suggested that the average level of profits achieved was higher than expected from capital invested in Britain (Inikori, 1981: 758–9; cf. Darity, 2000). James Wallace's *A General and Descriptive History of the Ancient and Present State of the Town of Liverpool* (1795), later reprinted many times, concluded that slave voyages in the decade 1783–93 made profits of over 30 per cent. Endorsements of a high profit rate came in *Liverpool and Slavery: An Historical*

Account of the Liverpool–African Slave Trade by a genuine 'Dicky Sam' (1884) and Gomer Williams's *History of the Liverpool Privateers and Letters of Marque with an Account of the Liverpool Slave Trade* (1897).

These antiquarian books presented unsophisticated, inaccurate calculations of slave trade profits: Gomer Williams erred in deducting the cost of trade goods from the returns on slave sales without allowing for overheads, thus exaggerating the scale of profits (Dumbell, 1931). Despite this cautionary note, the emphasis on large profits has permeated other studies. A carefully researched monograph of the early 1930s referred to the 'large fortunes [which] were to be made in the slave trade' (Wadsworth and Mann, 1931: 151). And a modern study of a hypothetical balance sheet of a slave trader presented before Parliament in 1788–9 calculated a profit ratio of 33 per cent (though it conceded that profits fluctuated over time and by the voyage) (Craton, 1974: 110–18).

Without providing any further detailed statistics, Eric Williams endorsed the figure of 30 per cent in average annual profits in the Liverpool slave trade in the decade after 1783 (1944: 36; the percentage has been repeated elsewhere: see P. Richardson, 1968: 21). He also made a general case for the contribution of slave trade earnings to Britain's industrial growth. To be sure, his analysis treated such profits as only one component – and perhaps not the most important one – that contributed to Britain's early industrialisation, but his statements on the theme were unequivocal. Thus: the profits from the slave trade 'provided one of the main streams of accumulation of capital in England which financed the Industrial Revolution' (E. Williams, 1944: 52). And: 'the triangular trade made an enormous contribution to Britain's industrial development. The profits from this trade fertilized the entire productive system of the country' (ibid.: 105). Williams also suggested that capital accumulation in Liverpool arising from the slave trade stimulated demographic growth in Lancashire and the manufacturing capacity of Manchester (ibid.: 63). These generalisations have proved influential but also highly contested. It is because of the impact of *Capitalism and Slavery* that the issues of whether slave trade profits were low, medium or high, whether they varied significantly over time and whether they really made an impact on Britain's early industrial revolution have led to ongoing debate among historians.

Concentrating to begin with on the scale of profits in the British slave trade, three main approaches have been followed, each of which has pitfalls. One has been to use surviving examples of slave traders' accounts for individual voyages. These give details of outward costs such as port fees, crew wages and payments to suppliers for export wares plus inward proceeds, including the profits on slaves and imported produce and the duties and shipping charges incurred for the voyage. Costs can then be deducted from gross profits and net gains estimated for the venture or an annual rate of return on investment calculated. The drawback of this procedure is that it has to rely on a relatively small surviving cache of accounts. A second approach has been to gather data on the number of slaves landed in the New World, their sale price and the volume of shipping that transported them, and to calculate profits from collating this material. Gaps in the records again make this an approach fraught with technical problems: the number of slaves landed in North America and the Caribbean has been revised frequently; slave sale prices have not yet been unearthed systematically from scattered sources; and care is needed to use the right type of shipping tonnage in making calculations. Thirdly, some historians have made assumptions about the size of slave trading firms, the degree of competition for slaves and the nature of the markets for black cargoes, and have sought to apply insights from economic theory to empirical data on the slave trade. These approaches need to be evaluated and their findings set out. This unavoidably necessitates a technical discussion about approaches to the sources. But it is important to do this thoroughly given the extensive debate on this topic: one cannot estimate the contribution of slave trading profits to early industrialisation in Britain unless one can demonstrate the scale of those earnings.

The case for moderate profits

Bradbury Parkinson, an accountant by profession, demonstrated how to interpret surviving slavers' accounts either by working out a profit-and-loss statement for each voyage or by comparing outsets and insets, that is, the original contributions and the eventual proceeds (Parkinson, 1951). In an article written with two coauthors, he examined some surviving records of Liverpool slave trading voyages to emphasise the great variety of financial outcomes for such ventures, the speculative nature of a risky triangular trade and the regular turnover of partnerships, all of which tended to reduce the high levels of profitability claimed by Williams and previous writers (Hyde, Parkinson and Marriner, 1952–3). The chief set of manuscripts used in this article, the accounts of the Liverpool merchant William Davenport and his partners, comprise the most comprehensive trading accounts for the British slave trade; they cover the period 1757–84. Further analysis of these records demonstrated that voyages sent out by Davenport and his firms made greater profits when trading with some parts of west Africa than with other regions, and that ventures which sold more than 55 per cent of the slave complements they had intended to purchase tended to be profitable and vice versa. Even such experienced hands, however, were not always successful; sometimes simultaneous voyages led to quite different outcomes. Of sixty-seven detailed inset and outset accounts in the Davenport Papers, forty-nine show a profit on the voyage and eighteen a loss. The seventy-four ventures studied accrued an annual average profit of 10.5 per cent or 8.1 per cent annually (D. Richardson, 1975, 1976).

Since these records covered the experience of only one firm and its multiple partnerships, a broader study of slave trade profits was needed. Roger Anstey supplied such an analysis by showing how to extract and adjust data from voyage accounts and link them with quotations on the price of slaves sold by the British in the Americas and the number of slaves landed in transatlantic areas. Following this approach, he concluded that profits in the British slave trade were 8.1 per cent in the period 1761–70, 9.1 per cent in 1771–80, 13.4 per cent in 1781–90, 13.0 per cent in 1791–1800 and 3.3 per cent in 1801–7. This pattern shows a rise in profits in the two decades after the American Revolution, in both war and peace years, followed by a serious decline in the last years of the legitimate trade. The aggregate rate of profit for the years from 1761 to 1807 was 9.5 per cent (Anstey, 1975a; 1975b: 38–57). Acceptance of a slightly higher estimate for the volume of the British slave trade led to a modest upward revision of this aggregate figure to 10.2 per cent (Anstey, 1976).

How do other profit estimates fit these figures? Between 1770 and

1792 profits per venture in the Bristol slave trade came to 7.6 per cent (D. Richardson, 1996: xxviii). A recent study of fifty-nine slave trading expeditions by a consortium of merchants based in London has arrived at an even more modest profit figure of 6 per cent for the period 1748–84 (Hancock, 1995: 423–4). Whether these profits were generally smaller than those gained earlier in the slave trade is difficult to say; the evidence is conflicting. The Royal African Company frequently complained about the profits they received and found it difficult to raise capital. On the other hand, the South Sea Company's slave deliveries to Spanish America c. 1714–36 appear to have generated larger profits than reported above for the late eighteenth century (Davies, 1957: 47–96; Palmer, 1980: 145–55). There is no clear trend in British slave trade profits prior to 1750, and it may be that insufficient source material is available to explore the matter further.

Recent debates on profits in the British slave trade

These estimates are clearly much lower than Eric Williams suggested. In the 1980s and 1990s they have been attacked by some historians as being too low and defended by others. The critics have focused narrowly on the period 1779–88, when it is argued that concentration occurred among Liverpool slave trading partnerships, with larger firms being more efficiently run than marginal firms; that Anstey's figure for average slave sales was too low at £36–7 per head and should be revised upwards to above £40, with slaves sold directly by the British in foreign territories fetching around £50; and that the volume of slave arrivals should also be increased. Reworking the profit calculations using these benchmarks points to a much higher rate of profit than the 10 per cent proposed by Anstey and Richardson (Inikori, 1981, 1983; Darity, 1985, 1989). Indeed, Joseph E. Inikori claims that the most efficient large merchants earned more than 50 per cent on their slave trading investment in the period 1779–88; and he implies that over time the trade *must have* operated according to such periods of short-run profits, though he concedes that he has no supporting evidence to sustain this hypothesis (Inikori, 1981: 745). Concentration on the 1780s was justified, according to this historian, because substantially higher profit margins were recorded then than in the decades immediately before and after. Larger, more efficient partnerships were included in the sample so that profit margins would not be understated by the inclusion of marginal firms (Inikori, 1983). A rider added to these points was that 10 per cent was too low an estimate for profitability in the slave trade given evidence that the general profit for eighteenth-century firms was around 13 per cent (Mirowski, 1982; Darity, 1989).

In response to these points, it has been argued that the high estimates of slave trade profits offered in these studies are misleading: they overestimate both the volume of slaves and the prices slaves sold for in the 1780s; they ignore time factors in estimating profits; and they are based on a small sample of voyages. Inikori's case for high abnormal profits in the British slave trade is based, for example, on only twenty-four voyages undertaken between 1765 and 1806 – and even they indicate the prevalence of highly variable returns (Inikori, 1981: 773). Moreover, the emphasis on concentration among firms in the Liverpool slave trade enabling them to exercise market power is misguided because the number of partnerships in the trade constantly fluctuated on a competitive basis (Anderson and Richardson, 1983: 715–19; 1985: 705). The general profit rate of 13 per cent cited for eighteenth-century firms is almost certainly too high. It also offers an unreliable comparison because it is based on a small sample of seventeen firms and does not use adjusted accounts (D. Richardson, 1989a: 495–8). We cannot be certain what eighteenth-century entrepreneurs considered to be a good profit. But since the standard rate of return on British government consols (a relatively risk-free investment) was 3.5 per cent for most of the eighteenth century, and governments were generally able to borrow money easily to support military endeavours, anything in the 8–10 per cent profit range would appear to be an acceptable return on capital invested.

The costs of transporting slaves also need to be emphasised along with the riskiness of the Guinea traffic. Average unit costs of transporting slaves rose from c. £5 per head in 1700 to £7 between the 1720s and 1750s, and to over £9 per head by the 1790s. Included in these costs were expenditures on fitting out vessels, the deployment of crew to control enslaved Africans and the subsistence requirements of slaves. Compared with the main commodities traded in the Atlantic basin, slaves were expensive to ship. The further the destination for slaves from the African coast, the greater the expense of shipment – something that should be considered when comparing the costs of slave deliveries to Barbados as opposed, to say, Jamaica, which was a thousand miles further away. The nature of the trade involved risk on all three legs of the voyage. The difficulties of timing voyages to secure good sales of exports on the African coast, the problem of getting slaves from the interior when wars and political changes occurred in the 'heart of darkness', the need to gauge slave deliveries to tap proceeds from the sale of plantation crops, the problems of extensive mortality on the Middle Passage, the loss of vessels to natural calamities or to enemy privateers in wartime, the worry of securing either full return cargoes in produce or a set of post-dated bills of exchange for reliable and prompt remittance – all these factors made the slave trade a precarious business proposition. Complete voyages usually took more than a calendar year, with little opportunity for productivity improvements in turn-around time in ports. These problems have led to reiteration of the point that annual net returns from the trade probably averaged less than 10 per cent on capital outlays (D. Richardson, 1987a).

It is now accepted that higher profit calculations for the slave trade have been based on unjustified assumptions made mainly by Inikori and Darity: they have been achieved by inflating the total of slaves delivered in the New World by British carriers and by overestimating the sale price of slaves (D. Richardson, 1987a, 1989a). The suggestions of an earlier study, applying theory rather than direct evidence, that the economic profits of the slave trade were not large appears to have been proven (though its other contention that the main financial gains were made by African suppliers, the 'fishers of men', needs empirical support) (Thomas and Bean, 1974). Detailed recent research on slave prices in the Caribbean suggests that they were near the £37 per head figure suggested by Anstey for the 1780s rather than above £40. The latter figure is seen to be inflated by failing to allow for the demographic composition of slave cargoes (in other words, assuming that mainly adult males, fetching high prices, were sold, rather than a mix of slaves) and by overestimating the number of slaves sold to foreign territories by British ship captains at marked-up prices (Behrendt, 1993: 106). A fully researched article on slave prices in the Caribbean is needed, however, to clear up the matter: existing price series have only scattered quotations and poor evidence on the sale price of slaves in foreign territories such as Spanish America and the French West Indies (e.g. Bean, 1975: 185–210).

The most careful recent calculations on profit levels in the slave trade, based on meticulous primary research, suggest that they reached 7.1 per cent between 1785 and 1790, 7.2 per cent in the period 1791–1800 and 7.5 per cent from 1801 to 1807. These figures overlap with the same periods as Anstey's calculations for the final years of legal British slaving activity. Apart from suggesting a smoother pattern over time, they are lower than the profits Anstey found for the 1790s but higher for the brief postlude to the British slave trade after 1800 (see above, 40). Interestingly, these recent calculations imply that profitability in the trade was little affected by Dolben's Act (1788) and the Slave Carrying Act (1799), the first parliamentary measures to restrict the number of slaves carried in relation to the tonnage and size of vessels. The conclusion of this recent research is that on average 'normal profits' of around 5 to 10 per cent were achieved in the final years of the legal British slave trade: the implication that the trade was a bonanza is largely a myth (Behrendt, 1993: 113).

Slave trade profits in relation to national income and industrial investment

If it has proven contentious to estimate profit levels in the final half-century of the British slave trade, the contribution of those proceeds to industrial investment is equally a matter of debate. Few original sources enable one to examine slave traders' investments in detail, though there are unexploited manuscripts that could be used for this purpose for selected individuals. It is difficult to show whether slave traders reinvested their profits in other trading enterprises or put the money into land, conspicuous consumption, transport investment or government stock; and also to what extent they might have drawn from non-trade sources for industrial investment. Slaving merchants operated in ad hoc partnerships that could change from voyage to voyage. Sometimes only the ship's 'husband' (or managing partner) remained involved in a sequence of Guinea ventures ostensibly under the same firm; the composition of the other partners, numbering anything up to seven people, frequently changed. This complicates the issue of looking at how gains from slave trading voyages might be invested.

Despite the problems with examining the flow of funds from the slave trade into the British economy, attempts have been made to resolve the issue. Adopting the perspective of neoclassical economics, and assuming that the supply of savings was perfectly inelastic and that all slave trading profits went into industrial investment rather than into consumption, Stanley L. Engerman has calculated the number of slaves carried by the British to the Americas, the profits achieved per slave, the level of British national income and the ratio of investment to income in order to determine the magnitude of the slave trade's contribution to investment. He concluded that trade had a modest annual average rate of return: the profits of transatlantic slaving amounted to much less than 1 per cent of British national income in the eighteenth century. Indeed, slave sale proceeds only came to £342,200 in 1770 of British national income amounting to £62.8 million. In other words, such profits comprised a mere 0.0054 per cent of national income in 1770, when the British slave trade was at its height in the 'silver age' of the sugar plantations (Engerman, 1972). On the assumption that the proportion of slave trading profits invested followed a national ratio of investment to national income of 7 per cent in 1800, another study found that slave trade profits for the second half of the eighteenth century comprised only 0.11 per cent of national investment; if all slave trading profits were invested, their contribution to total national investment would amount to 1.59 per cent (Anstey, 1975a: 22–4). Recently, an estimate of investment in the British slave trade c. 1790 of the order of £1.5 million per annum has led to the suggestion that annual profit levels in the trade were £150,000 and that one-third of these proceeds may have been invested. If so, slave trade profits probably made up less than 1 per cent of total domestic investment by the late 1780s (D. Richardson, 1998: 461). The conclusion drawn from these studies was that the contribution of slave trade earnings to the finance of British capital formation in the eighteenth century was small.

Table 2 *Slave trade profits as a percentage of national income, investment and commercial and industrial investment*

| | Slave trade profits (£ mil.) | National income (£ mil) | Investment (£ mil) | Comm./ind investment (£mil) | Slave trade profits as a % of | | |
					National income	Investment	Comm./ind investment
1688	0.179	48.0	1.4	0.14	0.37	13.0	128.0[a]
1710	0.110	57.4	2.3	0.28	0.19	4.8	39.3
1730	0.056	46.6	2.3	0.35	0.12	2.4	16.0
1750	0.215	51.7	3.1	0.54	0.42	6.9	39.8
1770	0.342	62.8	4.4	0.88	0.54	7.8	38.9

[a] No significance is to be attributed to this figure beyond the demonstration that commercial and industrial investment in 1688 was very small in a year of large slave trade profits; the number cannot be taken seriously.
Source: Solow (1985): 105.

This 'small ratios' argument has nevertheless been challenged by those who consider that Williams's arguments have been given short shrift. In a recalculation of the figures, Barbara L. Solow has taken data provided by Engerman on slave trade profits as a proportion of national income for selected years in the eighteenth century and worked out their percentage of total investment and commercial/ industrial investment (assuming that the latter comprised 20 per cent of the former in the late eighteenth century). This exercise, shown in table 2, demonstrated that the highest figure cited above for the ratio of slave trade profits to industrial investment is anything but small; it amounts to 10.8 per cent of capital formation.

Furthermore, the same profits for c. 1770 comprised nearly 8 per cent of total investment and no less than 39 per cent of commercial and industrial investment. The significance of this recalculation is striking: no single industry has achieved such high ratios in the modern United States. This argument was posited on the propensity of merchants to invest more than ordinary businessmen, and it assumed that all the profits were indeed channelled into industry and commerce. It therefore implied that there would be significant multiplier effects from slave trading and that the contribution of the slave trade to British industrialisation could have been very large: 'the profits of the slave trade and those derived from the West Indian colonies were quantitatively large compared with total British investment and with commercial and industrial investment, at the beginning of the Industrial Revolution' (Solow, 1985: 106). This conclusion is buttressed by noting that the annual 'resource increment' earned by the slave trade rose from c. £115,000 around 1770 to £379,200 in the 1790s, and that capital formation as a proportion of national income increased from 7 to 11 per cent between 1760 and the 1790s. This implies that slave trading profits constituted a greater share of total investment in 1800 than they did in 1770 (Blackburn, 1997: 542).

These abstract calculations are helpful in suggesting the potential magnitude of the contribution of slave trading gains to investment in Britain; they can tell us nothing about the channels of that investment. Of course, it might be argued that the destination of slave trade profits is not a major issue in the sense that wherever the money was used it contributed to British income (Solow and Engerman, 1987: 8–9). Yet it should be remembered that Solow's estimates of the ratio between slave trading profits, commercial and industrial investment, and total investment in the British economy were not offered in support of the Williams thesis: they only suggest what could have been the upper limit of the contribution of such gains (Solow, 1985: 106).

A critique of the methodology pursued in these studies can be offered. First, the calculation of the ratio of slave trade profits to national income is potentially skewed by reliance on estimates for profits from transatlantic slaving and calculations for British national income that are subject to regular revisions. Secondly, and more importantly, to look at the contribution of any sector or subsector of the economy in relation to national income or GNP is ultimately a narrow way of investigating the significance of trade and empire for the development of the British economy. It tells us something useful about a significant 'one-to-one' economic relationship generating small static gains but explains nothing about the dynamism or performance of that economy (see also McCloskey, 1994: 256). As Peter Mathias has suggested to me, it is rather like trying to measure the importance of ball bearings to the dynamic performance of a motor car by measuring their cost as a percentage of the capital cost of the vehicle. (A similar methodology has been used even more extensively in analysing the contribution of foreign capital to industrialisation and the ratio of manufactured exports to national income – both discussed in chapters 4 and 5 – and in several studies of 'social savings' connected with nineteenth-century canals and railways. A similar critique is relevant to these studies.) Certainly, one should broaden the discussion beyond the narrow focus on the profits of the Guinea trade. *Capitalism and Slavery*, of course, argued not merely for the input of slave trading proceeds to British industrial investment but also for the contribution made by the gains from slave labour on the plantations and the profits generated in other Atlantic trades. The next chapter considers these issues.

4

Slavery, Atlantic trade and capital accumulation

Another line of analysis in determining the contribution of transatlantic commerce to British economic growth emphasises the flow of capital from slavery and the Atlantic trading system into British industry. This linkage underpins many passages in Eric Williams's *Capitalism and Slavery*. A central concern is the argument that capital accumulation in Britain was boosted by the wealth produced by the Caribbean plantations, wealth based on the productivity of slaves and the profits of the sugar trade. This seems an obvious mode of enquiry, for the West Indian islands were the richest part of the first British Empire. It also seems reasonable to assume that entrepreneurs investing in the Caribbean, so far a distance from home, felt they could achieve better returns there than from channelling funds into domestic sectors of the British economy. The scale of West Indian wealth was recognised in the eighteenth century. Planters reckoned that the value of the British Caribbean islands amounted to £50–60 million in 1775 and to £70 million in 1789 (Drescher, 1977: 22–3). Contemporaries acknowledged the economic status of the West India plantocracy, notably the large numbers of absentees who lived in fine mansions with country estates rather than in the heat and dust of the Caribbean. Army and naval commanders, contemporary policy makers and the monarch himself all believed in the value of the sugar colonies to Britain and their contribution to national power (O'Shaughnessy, 2000). A well-known anecdote illustrates the point. King George III, when visiting Weymouth, came across a splendid equipage with outriders belonging to an absentee Jamaican planter, and exclaimed to his companion, the prime minister, 'Sugar, sugar, hey? all *that* sugar! How are the duties, hey, Pitt, how are the duties?' (Pares, 1960: 38).

Modern studies have also concluded that the wealth of the British Caribbean was substantial. Thus one estimate suggests that by 1770 annual profits of £800,000 accrued from Jamaican sugar production and £1.7 million from cultivating sugar throughout the British Caribbean (Ward, 1978: 209).

The economy of the British Caribbean in the late eighteenth century

The extent to which the wealth of the British Caribbean was still substantial by c. 1800, however, is a matter of historical controversy. Over seventy years ago Lowell Joseph Ragatz argued in *The Fall of the Planter Class in the British Caribbean, 1763–1833* (1928) that serious economic problems beset the Caribbean plantations from the end of the Seven Years War onwards. Relying extensively on the views of eighteenth-century planters, he provided much evidence to suggest that the wealth of the West Indies was in one important sense a mirage, for it depended on a British monopoly of markets at home and in British America that was paid for (via inflated sugar prices) by the consumers of sugar and rum. Ragatz was the first modern historian to marshal data supposedly showing the depression and declining profits in the British Caribbean sugar economy before slave emancipation rather than after (ibid.: 111–457; Higman, 1999: 71, 163). Taking his cue from Ragatz's arguments, Williams insisted in *Capitalism and Slavery* that many older West Indian sugar estates suffered from soil exhaustion, overproduction, debt and the waste of absentee ownership by the late eighteenth century; they therefore represented relatively poor investments for British merchants and planters (E. Williams, 1944: 145, 149–52). Certainly, difficulties occurred in the American War of Independence, when shipping lanes were interrupted in Caribbean waters, sugar prices and plantation profits declined and commercial depression hit the West Indies, with some older Jamaican properties falling into debt (Carrington, 1988).

Yet most historians consider that these problems were overcome by c. 1790. The population of the British West Indies grew by 40 per cent between 1750 and 1790; sugar production in the British Caribbean rose by nearly 11 per cent between 1770–3 and 1784–7;

productivity in sugar increased by around 14 per cent between the early 1770s and the mid-1780s; West Indian exports to Great Britain in the 1780s were nearly 9 per cent higher per capita constant value than they had been in the 1760s and early 1770s (McCusker, 1997: 310–30; see also Drescher, 1977). The West Indian plantation economy did not experience permanent difficulties until after 1815, when it faced world-wide competition in sugar production, falling sugar prices and rising duties, which led to a situation in 1830 where the average wholesale price of muscovado sugar on the London market, at 24 shillings per cwt, exactly equalled the import tariff on sugar – a dire situation for the plantocracy (Ward, 1985: 17–22; Green, 1976: 35–40, 414–15).

Recent research has discounted the notion of general economic decline in the British Caribbean by the time the British slave trade was abolished. Though there is no space here for a detailed technical discussion, the following points have been demonstrated. Soil exhaustion is a red herring, as sugar is not (unlike tobacco) a staple crop that inevitably depletes the fertility of the land, requiring new acreage to replace old. Technical improvements were made by a number of planters, including adapting steam engines to sugar mills, introducing new methods of cutting sugar, installing the latest designs in grinding mills and cultivating a new type of sugar cane that yielded more juice and a higher sugar content (Ragatz, 1928: 37–80, 199–202; Ward, 1985: 17–23; 1988; 1998: 429; Hancock, 1995: 150, 163; McCusker, 1997: 324–5). Profits were still being made on plantation accounts even in hard times during the French revolutionary and Napoleonic wars. This was still the case in the first two decades of the nineteenth century (Aufhauser, 1974; Ward, 1978, 1988). In Jamaica the labour productivity of slaves in planting sugar increased significantly, by 35 per cent between 1750 and 1830, allowing owners to achieve economies of scale (Ward, 1988: 192, 261).

Overproduction of sugar did occur in 1806 and 1807, on the eve of parliamentary abolition of the slave trade, and new evidence on sugar prices and estimated slave prices in Jamaica within a competitive international framework for the marketing of sugar indicates that a financial crisis did occur at this time for British sugar planters (Ryden, 2001). But these were temporary phenomena: upswings and downswings in the British Caribbean sugar economy had occurred before. Most contemporary politicians did not link over-production with abolition – a point that should be remembered by those who argue that the British abolished their slave trade for economic reasons. It is worth recalling that by 1807 the West Indian colonies still employed half the nation's long-distance shipping and supplied an eighth of Exchequer revenue via duties on imported produce; and the credit tied up in Caribbean trade and estates was 'a crucial element in the London financial market on which the government floated its war loans' (Ward, 1998: 427).

One should not paint too rosy a picture, of course, because by the early nineteenth century many planters with estates in Jamaica and Barbados complained about poor profits that 'barely covered oper-ating costs and were rarely sufficient to pay the interest on long-standing legacies and annuities' (Butler, 1995: 17). Yet by the 1820s, despite difficulties on some estates and a naturally declining slave population in most British West Indian islands, it is doubtful whether the British Caribbean economy had reached a state of unrecoverable failure. Certainly, there was no wholesale liquidation of plantations before slavery came to an end (Anstey, 1968: 314; Ward, 1985: 17–23, 1988).

Examining the period 1783–1807, Drescher established in *Econocide* that slavery had an expanding frontier in newer British possessions in the West Indies; that the British Caribbean retained its share of world sugar production; and that West India trade remained an important segment of total British overseas commerce (Drescher, 1977; cf. Eltis, 1987: 5–6). The conclusion drawn from the data presented was that abolition of the British slave trade came at a time of propitious economic trends for West Indian slavery. This turned the Ragatz–Williams argument on its head; instead of arguing that the decline of the sugar industry caused abolition, Drescher suggested that abolition caused decline. There are, to be sure, detailed critiques of these views and a robust response by Drescher, who suggested provocatively that the British Caribbean slave system in its final years (1828–32) was as valuable as it had been around 1750 (Minchinton, 1983, 1996; Carrington, 1984; Drescher, 1986). One historian occupies an isolated position in continuing to argue that West Indian economic decline was perva-sive in the late eighteenth century and that the abolition of the British slave trade marked a move towards free trade (Carrington,

1988, 1989). Most other historians take the opposite view, discounting any overall case for serious economic decline in the British Caribbean by 1807. The most recent summation of the plantation economy accepts a positive appraisal of the economic health of the British West Indies, implying that substantial wealth was still generated in that sector of the British Empire by the turn of the nineteenth century (Higman, 1996: 330–1). This did not necessarily mean that the British economy as a whole benefited, though it indicated that certain groups, notably merchants and planters, did well.

Yet, despite the wealth created by sugar and slaves, the contribution of plantation profits to industrial investment is not clear-cut. In some cases a direct connection existed. Among the families that transferred funds from their Jamaican sugar estates to domestic industrial enterprise were the Pennants and the Fullers. Richard Pennant, MP for Liverpool and later the first Lord Penrhyn, inherited 600 slaves and 8,000 acres of sugar plantations. He invested his money in slate quarries in North Wales that were part of the initial process of industrialisation in that area (Sheridan, 1973: 478–9; Craton, 1974: 153). Rose Fuller ran his family's Jamaican estates between 1734 and 1755 and later became MP for Rye and a prominent member of the West India interest. Other members of the family also had Caribbean connections. The Fullers put some of their capital into charcoal ironworks and gun foundries in the wealden part of Sussex (Crossley and Saville, 1991).

In other cases, the link between planter profits and industrial investment was tenuous. This can be illustrated by reference to two substantial families that amassed West India fortunes, the Pinneys and the Beckfords. John Pinney was worth £70,000 from his twenty-year residence in Nevis when he and his family quit that island in 1783 to live in Bristol and run a sugar commission business there. Pinney put some of his money into the new firm; he used the rest to take out loans on mortgages in the West Indies and to invest in government funds and landed property in England. But he did not channel his wealth into industry (Pares, 1950). A similar pattern can be found in the case of the Beckfords, perhaps the richest of all West India families. William Beckford was a millionaire who owned fourteen sugar plantations, more than a thousand slaves, and land and money in England. But he, too, did not invest much wealth in

British industry (Sheridan, 1964). It seems likely that Pinney and Beckford were more typical of absentee proprietors in this respect than the Pennants and the Fullers, though the number of case studies available from which one can generalise is small. The lures of land, government stocks, annuities and conspicuous consumption appear to have been higher priorities for West India planters than industrial investments, or, as Richard Pares put it, 'there seem to have been more Fonthills than factories among them, and more overdrafts and protested bills than either' (Pares, 1936–7: 130).

The wealth of Jamaica in the eighteenth century

It used to be argued that a planter oligarchy amassed large fortunes in the West Indies and repatriated their wealth, using it to buy landed estates. Their financial standing boosted their social status, the argument continues, and this facilitated marriages into the upper echelons of British society and influence on imperial policies (Pitman, 1917: 21, 39–40). During the eighteenth century, the West India interest became a significant lobbying group at Westminster and its members were not strangers to commercial opulence. Indeed, in 1774 Edward Long stated that most property owners in Jamaica 'had flocked to Britain and North America, beyond the example of former times, and drained their incomes from the island'. Yet the Abbé Raynal, in *A Philosophical . . . History . . . of the East and West Indies* (1788), suggested that the British Caribbean islands owed something like £16 million to Britain at the time of the American Revolution. Thus, contemporary commentators were divided on the extent to which the wealth of the West Indies led to profits accruing to merchants and planters in Great Britain or, on the contrary, to accumulated debts.

A leading authority on the Caribbean in the first half of the twentieth century was inclined to agree with Long: 'the wealth of the British West Indies did not all proceed from the mother country; after some initial loans in the earliest period which merely primed the pump, the wealth of the West Indies was created out of the profits of the West Indies themselves, and with some assistance from the British taxpayer, much of it found a permanent home in Great Britain' (Pares, 1960: 50). This comment suggests that absentee proprietors extracted their money invested in the Caribbean; but in fact the degree to which their wealth was repatriated is by no means easy to establish. Possibly it was not until the era of slave emancipation that many planters, worried about liquidating their assets, rushed to funnel their money out of their West Indian estates back to Britain (Davies, 1960–1: 110). In the future, one hopes that economic historians will explore these matters in greater depth to ascertain the scale of the mortgage debt in the British Caribbean over time and the extent and timing of the repatriation of wealth from that region.

Richard B. Sheridan has examined wealth patterns in the Caribbean in detail. Examining the wealth recorded in Jamaican inventories and adjusting for the absence of realty in such records, he has presented data showing that total inventory valuation, including slaves, increased nearly two-and-a-half times from an average of £3,819 in 1741–5 to £9,361 in 1771–5. This rise was almost entirely associated with slaveholding: slaves doubled in number between the two periods and their average value increased by 76 per cent. Extrapolating from these findings, Sheridan calculated that by 1775 the valuation of sugar estates in Jamaica alone, which accounted for half of British investment in the Caribbean, amounted to some £18 million sterling (about £9 billion in today's money), with an annual net income to Jamaicans and British merchants and absentees of £1.5 million. He concluded that 8–10 per cent of British income c. 1775 consisted of funds flowing inwards from the Caribbean, and that the percentage was higher before the War of Independence (Sheridan, 1965). Sheridan's figure for Jamaican wealth on the eve of the American Revolution more than doubled a slightly earlier estimate of £7.5 million for the capital and value of sugar estates in the island (Davies, 1960–1: 107).

Robert P. Thomas responded to this assessment in a critical fashion. Emphasising the costs of imperial defence and the inflation of sugar prices by preferential tariffs, he argued contrariwise that the colonies were a net drain on British resources and absorbed money that would have been better deployed elsewhere. British consumers paid higher prices for sugar because of import duties imposed in a protected market; they would have purchased their sugar more cheaply if free trade had been in operation. Calculating the social rate of return by the Caribbean colonies to Britain – in other words, the costs of imperial defence subtracted from the profits accruing in the islands – Thomas arrived at a figure of £660,750 or less than 2 per cent on invested capital. By contrast, the rate of return on British government consols was 3.5 per cent at this time. This neo-Smithian argument viewed the colonies as retarding British economic growth because the capital invested in the West Indies could have earned higher returns if invested elsewhere – for instance, in government funds as implied above (Thomas, 1968). Another historian supported this approach by claiming that high import prices meant that the colonies were a drain on Great Britain's resources: British income in the period 1768–72 would have been greater if the British Caribbean islands had belonged to another European power; and more capital was flowing out of Britain to the West Indies than coming back. In this scenario, the only plausible reason for continuing British investment in the Caribbean lay in the private interests of merchants and planters, bolstered by effective lobbying at Westminster (Coelho, 1973). Sheridan restated his original case by arguing that, inter alia, Thomas's calculations neglected the role of invisibles in the balance of payments between the British West Indies and the mother country, and also provided an inaccurate ratio of non-sugar wealth to sugar wealth in Jamaica (Sheridan, 1968).

This debate was an interesting attempt to provide a cost–benefit analysis. It raised the question of whether the wealth generated in the British West Indies added to private profits at home and helped to redistribute the gains from staple products from consumers to producers. It also tackled the difficulty of estimating the defence costs of the colonies in the Caribbean, the cockpit of European international rivalry in the eighteenth century (Engerman, 1975: 334; Blackburn, 1997: 532–5). Yet the debate failed to reach a consensus, perhaps because of inherent flaws in the arguments. Thomas's analysis applied more to specific commercial and imperial policies followed by British governments than to the value of the West Indies per se. His interpretation failed to note the positive effect of colonial expansion on British incomes in the first place and the necessity, whether or not colonies were involved, for the British to maintain a costly naval presence in the Caribbean to counteract French maritime rivalry. Moreover, he biased the data in favour of his own interpretation by doubling the profits gained from West

Indian trade and offering too high an estimate of the defence and administration costs of the British Caribbean. Sheridan, for his part, probably overestimated the ease of extracting money tied up in mortgage and plantation debts in the West Indies (Pares, 1960: 44–6; Darity, 1982a: 292, 322; Duffy, 1987: 20; Solow, 1985: 106–9). Another historian, arguing that Sheridan's data on Jamaican wealth were too high, arrived at an aggregate wealth figure of £15,808,300 for Jamaica in the early 1770s (Coclanis, 1990: 258). But this re-evaluation neglected to consider Jamaican wealth outside the sugar sector and arrived at a figure for per capita wealth by using an inflated population figure for the white Jamaican population in 1774 (Burnard, 2001).

Trevor Burnard has recently revived the debate on the wealth of Jamaica. Undertaking detailed work on Jamaican inventories and parish registers, he has produced better estimates of wealth, income and product by looking at the percentage of wealth holders who were inventoried in Jamaica and how representative they were of the total number of wealth holders dying each year. His conclusion is more in line with the higher estimates of Jamaican wealth provided by contemporaries than with the modern assessments outlined above. For 1774, Burnard's data suggest that the wealth of Jamaica was £28,040,217, with annual income coming to £5,960,023. This gives a wealth-to-income ratio of 4.7:1. These are much higher figures than one finds in comparable data for the thirteen British colonies in mainland North America at that time. Assuming that the ratio of British Caribbean wealth to Jamaican wealth was the same as the ratio of British West Indian exports to Jamaican exports, the total wealth of the British possessions in the Caribbean in 1774 was £51,926,327, of which Barbados contributed £6,127,327, the ceded islands £6,335,000 and the Leewards £11,424,000 (Burnard, forthcoming). The figure for the total wealth of the West Indies in 1774 exceeds that calculated by Sheridan over thirty years before; it defends the figures estimated by contemporaries; but it is less than a rough modern estimate which suggested that the British West Indian estates were worth £50 million in 1775 (Pitman, 1931: 271). Since these were private returns on capital, the potential was there for investment; the social costs of colonial defence did not fall, in the main, on planters (Hudson, 1992: 195).

Profits from the colonies and imperial trade and capital accumulation in Britain

Immanuel Wallerstein revived the debate on a broader scale by looking at the whole of Europe's trading connections with the outside world from the age of discovery until the era of Enlightenment. Writing from a Marxist perspective, he depicts a 'world system' of trade that emerged in the early modern era, a system in which wealth generated in the 'periphery' (i.e. the colonies) became a vital source of capital accumulation in the 'core' (i.e. the metropolitan centre of empire) (Wallerstein, 1980). His evidence to support these grand themes, however, is almost certainly overstated. A re-examination of the topic has constructed estimates to show that commerce with the 'periphery' generated funds sufficient to finance only 15 per cent of gross investment expenditures during the Industrial Revolution (O'Brien, 1982 and his exchange of comments with Wallerstein, *Economic History Review*, 2nd ser., 35, 1982: 580–5). In a wide-ranging discussion of the impact of the 'periphery' on European economic development in the three centuries after 1450, Patrick O'Brien has argued that external trade was only a small proportion of Europe's economic activity and that most industries did not depend upon imported raw materials: 'since Britain industrialised before the rest of Europe there is no reason to claim that if western Europe had been forced to manage without imported sugar, coffee, tea, tobacco, and cotton, its industrial output could have fallen by a large percentage. A decline of not more than 3 or 4 per cent in the industrial output of the core would seem to be the likely *short-run* effect from a total cut-off of imports.' O'Brien's pungent conclusion was that 'for the economic growth of the core, the periphery was peripheral' (O'Brien, 1982: 12, 18). Other historians have argued that sugar did not furnish a sufficiently large total output to be a major contributor to the savings that funded the Industrial Revolution (Eltis, 1997: 129; Engerman, 1998). These arguments in favour of 'small ratios' parallel those presented in chapter 3 on the profits of the slave trade, and my comments on the methodology applied are also relevant here (see above, 45–8). Future studies using this approach will need fuller investigation of the composition of trade, links between industries and various multiplier effects, but current scholarship has not vindicated Wallerstein's expansive claims (Darity, 1992a: 252–5).

It is equally difficult to prove that merchant capital amassed from colonial commerce was decisive for British industrial growth. Profits earned in the Atlantic trades were invested in shipbuilding, snuff mills, sugar refineries, glassworks, ironworks, textiles, coal mines and other industrial enterprises in London and the major west coast outports and their hinterlands (Hyde, 1971: 19–21; Devine, 1976, 1977; Beckett, 1981; K. Morgan, 1996a: 22). Bristol, for example, had twenty sugar refineries clustered in its city centre in the mid-eighteenth century plus a number of snuff mills in the outlying suburbs; but it also catered for the export trade with copper and brass works and glass houses. These were among the businesses that made it the 'metropolis of the west'. Mercantile capital amassed in colonial trade at Bristol percolated into mining enterprises in South Wales and Shropshire (Minchinton, 1954; K. Morgan, 1993a: 97–8, 102–3; 1998). Liverpudlians invested in salt works, sugar refineries, breweries and distilleries and in copper, glass and iron smelting in Liverpool and south Lancashire, especially after 1750 (Hyde, 1971; Langton, 1983). Yet from surviving records it is impossible to establish what proportion of merchants' investment in industry originated from overseas trade rather than from sources such as banking, insurance, land and government stock. Furthermore, it is likely that many merchants who did business on the basis of 'gains-from-trade', by buying goods cheaply and selling them dear, did not generate sufficient profits to stimulate industry in a significant way (Kindleberger, 1975: 647–8). And since important branches of Atlantic trade involved British merchants acting as factors for tobacco, sugar and rice planters, it could be argued that such merchants had to use all their financial resources to maintain the flow of trade (Pares, 1936–7: 130).

The case of Glasgow is instructive, for it is the one British port where this matter has received full attention. In the forty years before the American Revolution, Glasgow thrived on the success of the Chesapeake tobacco trade. Great wealth accrued from this commerce to the city's tobacco lords. Merchant investment was significant in Glasgow and west-central Scotland in industrial ventures such as textiles, iron, sugar refining, glassworks and leather manufactories. For instance, a group of tightly knit Glasgow tobacco importers gained control over the glassmaking industry in the west of Scotland. Sugar-processing and the rope and sailcloth industries in the Clyde region were also dominated by Glasgow tobacco merchants. Despite substantial merchant involvement in industry, however, no substantial flow of capital from the tobacco trade to the cotton industry occurred in Scotland: by c. 1795 only about 17 per cent of the value of cotton firms north of the border was financed by colonial traders. And there was no straightforward flow of trading profits generally into the Scottish domestic economy. Glasgow's position as an entrepôt in the tobacco trade probably accounted for such a limited multiplier effect, but these findings also fit our knowledge of the modest fixed capital requirements of the early stages of industrialisation (Devine, 1975: 43–6; 1976: 12–13).

A recent attempt to revive the significance of foreign capital flows for Britain's industrialisation has foundered on misinterpretation of evidence. The case in favour of the connection constructed a balance-of-payments account and estimated national income to argue that Britain's net foreign debts increased from £2 million in 1710 to £103 million by the 1780s, and that this large increase in capital flows provided nearly one-third of total investment in the economy (Brezis, 1995). This conclusion has nevertheless been refuted convincingly by a careful recalculation of the figures to include earnings in the multilateral trades – a significant part of the current account – plus better estimates of shipping tonnages and freight rates. This revision concluded, on the contrary, that Britain had an accumulated indebtedness in the 1770s and 1780s of £18 million and £31 million respectively. The verdict reached in the revision was that England's foreign debts c. 1770 were £10–20 million at most, and that therefore foreign capital did not play a major part in England's industrialisation (Nash, 1997).

5
British exports and
transatlantic markets

Another way of looking at the connection between Atlantic trade and British economic development is to emphasise demand both in the Americas and within Britain as a major spur to exports from England and Scotland – a theme hinted at, though not fully discussed, in sections of *Capitalism and Slavery* that deal with links between British industry and the triangular trade (E. Williams, 1944: 98–107). This chapter broadens that approach by considering Britain's export growth in a variety of transatlantic trades, not just the slave trade. It explores the links between burgeoning exports and the growth of domestic manufacturing. Concentration on exports to transatlantic regions is justified by the fact that no other overseas market for British wares grew so significantly in the eighteenth century. Over three-quarters of British goods sent across the Atlantic were manufactured commodities rather than raw materials or foodstuffs, so the links between British industry and exports are highly relevant for our discussion.

The outcome of the American demand for British export wares can be seen in the increasing value of such trade over time. Though there are no continuous series of trade figures for the late seventeenth century, data on London's exports show that they increased from an average value of £163,000 in 1663–9 to £410,000 in 1699–1701, increasing from 8 to 15 per cent of total exports from the metropolis (Davis, 1954). The trade grew rapidly on a national basis thereafter. The annual average value of English exports and re-exports to transatlantic regions was £1,218,000 in 1699–1701, increasing modestly to £2,283,000 in 1722–4 (Davis, 1962–3). The annual average level reached £3,009,000 in 1766–70, and then more than trebled, from £3,540,000 in 1781–5 to £11,164,000 in

1796–1800 (Schumpeter, 1960: 17). Since these customs figures are in 'official' rather than current prices, they are a good index of trade volume. The proportion of exports dispatched to transatlantic areas underscores the significance of North American and West Indian markets for British exports in the eighteenth century (see above, 18–20). The accelerating growth depicted by these data points to an export boom to transatlantic areas between 1783 and 1800, something appropriately labelled the 'Americanisation' of British exports (Mathias, 1983: 91).

American consumers were the recipients of an Atlantic extension of Georgian Britain's consumer revolution, in which advertisements, merchants' displays and news of other people's acquisitions fuelled the colonists' desire for British goods. Colonial American inventories reveal the increasing range of consumer goods attracting purchases by the mid-eighteenth century. The growth in the export trade gave North American customers more choice in their consumption of British manufactured wares; and the fact that similar products were available in most of the thirteen colonies and states meant that consumer behaviour in North America became more standardised as the market for imported goods expanded (Breen, 1986, 1988). A great many retailers and shopkeepers ran stores in the American colonies. These served as the conduit for the sale of British wares to urban and backcountry customers (Doerflinger, 1988; Shammas, 1990: 266–85).

Export growth was achieved despite several potential problems. The dry goods trade had a boom-and-bust character caused by seasonal and yearly fluctuations in the supply of goods, cyclical changes in the demand for manufactured commodities and difficulties caused by exchange rate fluctuations, overextension of credit by British exporters, the problem of collecting debts from American customers when cash was scarce and the impact of eighteenth-century warfare on trade (Doerflinger, 1986: 85–97, 171–3, 262–7; K. Morgan, 1993a: 111–19). As a result, the volume of exports sometimes varied alarmingly from one year to the next. There were many peaks and troughs in the export trade to transatlantic areas because of the difficulties mentioned. Interruptions to trade also occurred in North American non-importation boycotts in the years 1765–6, 1768–70 and 1774–6, when Philadelphia, New York, Boston and Charleston were closed for long stretches of time to British vessels. Trade was also disrupted during the American War of Independence. British vessels ceased sailing to North America apart from voyages to New York City and Philadelphia while they were under British military control. During wartime British ships on voyages to and from the West Indies frequently sailed in fleets under convoy in an attempt to avoid French, Spanish and American privateers. Further disruption of trade patterns occurred after Britain went to war with revolutionary France in 1793.

Despite these difficulties, British exports to transatlantic regions increased significantly in the second half of the eighteenth century; they also became more varied to satisfy consumer tastes. Until 1750 woollens dominated English exports as they had done for centuries. In 1699–1701 woollens comprised 85 per cent of the value of all domestic manufactured exports. By 1752–4 they constituted 62 per cent. By 1772–4, their share had fallen to 49 per cent (Davis, 1962–3). In the quarter-century before the American Revolution, the range of exports widened to include a more extensive range of textiles and a variety of manufactures (notably metalware) that were probably concentrated at the top and bottom ends of the price range (Davis, 1967: 4, 18–20; Price, 1984: 35; 1998: 102). Between 1750 and 1775 there was a surge in the value of cotton piece goods exported, and greatly increased transatlantic markets for linen: these fabrics were suitable for shirts, trousers, gowns and underwear. In the first half of the eighteenth century, the English linen industry was very small and provided virtually no exports; the cotton industry was also modest in size, with limited export sales. This growth in the transatlantic markets for cottons, linens and metalware can be regarded as central to the surge of production in those industries in mid-Georgian Britain (Inikori, 1993: 25).

Among various manufactured wares exported in much greater quantities after 1750 were nails, buttons, copper and brass wares, buckles, clocks, mirrors, locks, hinges, tableware, hardware, firearms, cutlery and glassware. Table 3 shows that by 1770 about half of all English exports of ironware, copper and brass pots and pans, earthenware, glassware, window glass, printed cotton and linen goods, silk goods and flannels were sent to the colonies plus two-thirds or more of all exports of cordage, sailcloth, iron nails, beaver hats, wrought leather, linen and Spanish cloth woollen goods. A

Table 3 *Selected English exports sent to British America, 1770*

Commodity	Quantities exported to British America		Percentage of total exported from England
Coal	6,085	chaldrons	2.8
Pilchards	160	hogsheads	0.8
White salt	11,024	pounds	23.0
Refined sugar	12,062	cwt	31.7
Wrought brass	8,073	cwt	25.2
Wrought copper	13,778	cwt	55.3
Wrought iron	130,687	cwt	59.8
Lead and shot	1,651	fodders	9.3
Wrought leather	249,640	lb	85.4
Tin	216	cwt	31.7
Beaver hats	10,790	dozen	69.4
Cordage	11,837	cwt	65.6
Glassware and earthenware	2,742,253	pieces	47.9
Window glass	4164 cwt 34 qr 252 lb		48.3
Iron nails	24,147	cwt	76.5
Tanned leather	408	cwt	5.2
Fustians	5,116	pieces	15.7
Linen	88,072	pieces	79.2
Sailcloth	768,650	ells	77.5
Wrought silk	30,978	pounds	57.2
Printed cotton and linen	155,789	yards	58.9
Double bays	17,812	pieces	19.9
Single bays	8,702	pieces	12.3
Long cloths	5,176	pieces	15.8
Short cloths	18,249	pieces	36.8
Spanish cloths	1,985	pieces	70.4
Kerseys	4,715	pieces	25.8
Welsh plains	421,792	goads	84.7
Perpets and serges	76,396	pounds	2.2
Flannel	346,740	yards	42.6
Men's worsted	28,806	dozen pairs	34.9
Stockings stuffs	1,225,750	pounds	14.8

Sources: McCusker and Menard (1985): Table 13.2, 284; and Customs 3/ 70, Public Record Office, London.

glance at surviving merchants' invoices or advertisements for British wares in American newspapers will indicate the complexity and variety of this 'empire of goods' (Breen, 1986; Doerflinger, 1988: 166, 169). The chief characteristic of the second phase of export growth after 1783 was an expanded volume of exports with a narrower base centred on the renewed dominance of textiles. Between 1784–6 and 1794–6 all textiles contributed 57 per cent and metalwares 20 per cent to the growth of British exports. From 1794–6 to 1804–6 the respective figures were 82 per cent (with cottons comprising 73 per cent) and 7 per cent (Crouzet, 1980: 62–3).

The transatlantic demand for British exports

The substantial increase in commodities shipped across the Atlantic was fuelled by rapid population growth, denser internal settlement stretching to frontier areas, rising living standards and changing tastes in North America and the West Indies. The population of those parts of North America that became the United States multiplied twentyfold from 275,000 people in 1700 to 5.3 million in 1800, an incredible upsurge that T. R. Malthus in *An Essay on the Principle of Population* referred to as 'a rapidity of increase almost without parallel in history' (1826, vol. I: 517). During the eighteenth century, the per capita income of white settlers rose at an annual rate of between 0.3 and 0.6 per cent – not spectacular by modern standards but comparable to growth rates in Britain and France at that time (McCusker and Menard, 1985: 55–60, 268). By the 1770s anything up to 30 per cent of the per capita income of any one North American colony was spent on imported goods, of which three-quarters were British export wares (Bowen, 1996: 117). Between 1700 and 1790 the predominantly black population of the British Caribbean quadrupled from 148,000 to 570,000 people, while by the 1770s the net worth of white settlers in Jamaica amounted to £1,200 per person (McCusker and Menard, 1985: 154; McCusker, 1997: 312, 329). Rising prosperity based on slavery, sugar, and mercantile and planter wealth enabled white colonists to buy a wide array of consumer goods.

Several advantages helped Britain to tap these funds. The Navigation Acts provided a large protected market for British manufactures within the empire (see above, 13–14). Competition from homespun industry was reduced by high labour costs in the colonies and by government restrictions on the American manufacture of products such as cloth, hats, nails, earthenware, steel and refined iron: the colonies were expected to serve as protected markets for the export industries of Great Britain. British merchants also offered attractive terms to American customers. They conducted trade mainly through the use of commercial credit rather than borrowing by bond or from banks, and allowed a credit period of nine to twelve months, sometimes even fifteen or eighteen months, before payment for goods was required (Price, 1980: 44–123; K. Morgan, 1993a: 110–11). These long credits, discussed more fully in chapter 6, were usually more generous than those provided by European merchants.

British exporters also became familiar over time with the varied tastes of colonial consumers, and generally sold textiles and other wares that were cheaper and of better quality than similar goods produced in America. Great attention was paid to different figures, colours and patterns among textiles to suit changing fashions. Ornamental, colourful textiles and porcelain had been stimulated by the popularity of oriental designs, manifest in Indian printed cottons and silks, and by the European vogue for chinoiserie in furniture, china and textile design from the mid-seventeenth century onwards (Berg, 1994: 126, 129, 133). Merchants supplied pattern cards illustrating the colour and price of cottons, linens, silks and woollens so that American merchants could show them to their customers and then order goods with exact attention to what was required (K. Morgan, 2000a). Given the superiority and cheapness of British articles over those manufactured by the Dutch and the French, it is not surprising that some American merchants maintained contacts with British firms during the War of Independence and that British manufactured products were so much in demand in the USA after 1783, when European firms were trying to capture that market (e.g. Wadsworth and Mann, 1931: 148–67; Devine, 1975: 165; Price, 1980; K. Morgan, 1993a: 89–127; 2000a). American domestic textile production could not fully compete with imported British and Indian textiles in the period 1780–1800 partly because the imported goods were cheaper and better in quality and partly because spinning and weaving had not yet been mechanised in the United States.

The interplay between external and internal factors underlying the growth of British exports is difficult to separate out: upswings and downswings in the cycle of exports were subject to multiple economic influences (O'Brien and Engerman, 1991: 207). Clearly, though, the demand for British manufactured goods was not entirely an exogenous affair, for exports sent to American markets were stimulated by increased purchasing power in both Britain and the Caribbean. David Richardson has emphasised the growth of the slave trade and sugar consumption in meeting this demand. Sugar and its byproducts, rum and molasses, were the most valuable British imports from anywhere in the world in the eighteenth century. Between 1748 and 1776 sugar imports doubled from 900,000 to 1.8 million cwt; sugar consumption doubled to reach a per capita level of 25 lb; and average gross revenues from sugar sales also doubled, from £1.6 million to £3.2 million. Such extensive demand from British consumers acquiring a sweet tooth through drinking sugar with tea, coffee, cocoa and chocolate was probably aided by rising wages in the industrialising areas of the country and by constraints on the production of other beverages such as beer. Incomes accruing from expanding sugar sales in Britain provided the impetus to expand the slave trade to maintain the output of the plantations (given the heavy mortality rate among slaves in the West Indies). The annual number of slaves shipped in British vessels rose from around 25,800 between 1749 and 1755 to reach a peak of 43,500 in the period 1763–75. Booming sugar sales also induced a demand for exports of clothing (mainly linen at this stage) and plantation equipment destined for the West Indies. In addition, surpluses derived from trade between mainland America and the Caribbean paid for about one-quarter of the goods that North Americans bought from Britain between 1750 and 1770. It has been argued, therefore, that Caribbean-based demand may have accounted for about 35 per cent of the growth of total British exports between 1748 and 1776, and for about 12 per cent of the increase in British industrial output in the quarter-century before the American Revolution (D. Richardson, 1987b). Unfortunately, no historian has systematically analysed the interconnections between transatlantic demand for British exports and the growth of the sugar economy and the slave trade in the post-1783 period to determine the extent to which British industrial production was stimulated by the derived demand for enslaved African labour during the final phase of the legal British traffic in slaves.

Industrial output and exports

To evaluate whether this varied demand acted as a trigger for British economic growth, one needs data on the proportion of industrial output that was exported and, in particular, dispatched across the Atlantic. This is a tricky matter because we lack accurate production estimates for most branches of British industry in the eighteenth century: one has to gather data from scattered, incomplete sources on an industry-by-industry basis. It seems that the proportion of industrial output exported rose from about one-quarter in 1700 to around one-third in 1800, and during the same century exports accounted for 40 per cent of the increase in industrial output (Cole, 1981: 39–40; Engerman, 1994: 189). A recent quantitative study has boosted the significance of exports in relation to industrial production. Javier Cuenca Esteban has provided data showing that the share of industrial exports in industrial output rose almost continuously from 1723 until 1851, and that between 50 and 79 per cent of additional industrial production (calculated as incremental ratios based on constant prices) could have been exported in the period 1780–1801 (Esteban, 1997). From 1660 to 1815 possibly 30–40 per cent of all additional industrial output manufactured in Britain was exported (O'Brien and Escosura, 1998: 59). The ratio of exports to production shifted significantly over time, with successive changes between the proportion of the wool, cotton and iron industries in domestic and foreign markets (Crouzet, 1980: 85–8), but Esteban's overall figures (derived from new annual estimates of Britain's domestic export values in constant and current prices) are striking evidence of the significant growth in manufactured exports in the eighteenth century. Given the increasing American orientation of British exports, they also indicate the 'pull' of American consumers demanding manufactured wares from British suppliers.

There was, of course, considerable variation among individual industries in the share of production sent abroad. Exports of copper and brass – both comparatively small industries at this time – accounted for around 40 per cent of production on the eve of the American Revolution, while the nailmaking trades in Birmingham and the Black Country were said to export three-quarters of their product to British America by the 1760s. Two branches of textiles were also very reliant on exports. The woollen industry sold 45 per cent of its product abroad c. 1695 and in 1772, and about 55 per cent in 1799. Indeed the Yorkshire woollen industry exported some 72 per cent of its production in 1772, when Yorkshire was supplying approximately half of Britain's cloth exports and when nearly one-third of all woollen exports were sent to the colonies. The woollens in demand overseas included broad cloths, blankets, bays and Rochdale goods, worsteds, kerseys and half thicks. By 1800, the United States took 40 per cent of British wool textile exports, including well over half of the woollens and worsteds produced in Yorkshire (Wilson, 1973: 230, 243–4; Crouzet, 1980: 87–9; K. Morgan, 1996a: 26). The most significant industry with a high ratio of exports to production was cotton, which sold 50 per cent of its manufacture abroad in 1760 and 62 per cent in 1801 (Crafts, 1985: 143). This was the most rapidly rising British industry in the second half of the eighteenth century. American consumers particularly bought cotton and linen printed cloths and plain calicoes, fabrics that were especially suitable for warmer climates. Cotton goods were also used in exchange for slaves on the African coast.

Other industries present a less striking picture. English and Scottish linen exports accounted for, at most, 20 per cent of production by the 1770s, while the iron trades – important suppliers of colonial markets at mid-century – depended on exports for 20 per cent of their gross product by the 1770s and for 24 per cent in 1801 (Price, 1979: 229–32, 239; Crafts, 1985: 143; K. Morgan, 1996a: 26–7).

Exports and British economic growth

This analysis reveals the complex relationship between exports and economic growth and brings us to the heart of the debate on the respective roles of home and foreign demand at the beginnings of industrialisation. Historians who see the home market as the main source of growth can argue that only one industry (cotton) ever had more than half of its product exported in the eighteenth century – and then only in certain years in the period 1760–1801. In this line of analysis, cotton appears to be the one British industry that was essentially nourished by transatlantic trade (O'Brien, 1990: 167–8). The ratio of exports to national output fluctuated during the eighteenth century but peaked at 15.7 per cent only in 1801 – a much lower ratio of exports to GNP than occurred in the late Victorian period (Crafts, 1985: 131). Estimates of sectoral growth rates in eighteenth-century British industry show a steady rise in the output of various industries, including many that did not provide significant exports (soap, coal, leather, brewing, building and construction are examples) (ibid.: 145). This broadly based industrial output for the domestic market underscores the significance of home demand for economic growth. Agricultural productivity has been also seen as lying behind increased domestic demand in the first half of the eighteenth century (John, 1965).

A strong case can nevertheless be made for exports as a generator of growth in the second half of the eighteenth century in general and in its last two decades in particular (bearing in mind the caveat that exports' contribution to national output was never as great as in the post-1850 period). The increase in the quantity and variety of manufactured exports encouraged the development of the non-agricultural sector of the British economy and diversified Atlantic trade so that it was no longer 'import-led' as had been the case in the early years of British overseas colonisation. British merchants vended goods to America at a critical period in the mid-eighteenth century when long-standing European markets for woollens and worsteds were in decline and when exports, rather than agricultural incomes, were becoming a major stimulus to manufacturing (Davis, 1962–3: 102–3; O'Brien, 1985; Lee, 1986: 115–16). Without markets in the colonies, British industries would not have had the incentive for rapid expansion at that time. This, in fact, was the theme of Ralph Davis's concluding speculations in *The Rise of the English Shipping Industry in the Seventeenth and Eighteenth Centuries* (1962): 'if colonial America had been lost or whittled away; if during its lifetime it had been a Dutch commercial province; where would have been the merchant fortunes, the crown revenues, accumulated in England through colonial trade? Where would the English industries have found room for massive expansion? A much poorer, a much less industrialised England in mid-century; would this have provided a firm basis for take-off into Industrial Revolution?' (p. 394). A more recent assessment has concurred with these speculations by suggesting that the returns would have been less if the resources put into exports had been directed into other sectors of the British economy (Lee, 1986: 118–19).

Thus the large trading basin of the British Empire became vital after 1750 for industrialising areas in Britain because it gave added incentive for manufacturers in Yorkshire, Lancashire and the Midlands to quicken the productivity of textiles, metalware and hardware through extra employment, the division of labour and improved commercial organisation (Davis, 1962: 391–4; Inikori, 1992). These developments are a firm indication of an economy 'on the move', responding to increased demand and utilising surplus labour eager to earn rising wages. They underpin the notion that business expertise and product innovation responded to the growth of market opportunities. They imply that export expansion was quicker than domestic demand and that it helped to break through the 'balanced' threshold of demand that existed in the home market (Berrill, 1960: 354). The surges in export demand may have stimulated productivity and innovation in English regions, given the concentration by c. 1780 of woollen textiles for export in the West Riding of Yorkshire, of cottons in south Lancashire and of metalware and hardware in Birmingham and the Black Country (Hudson, 1992: 182).

Indeed, an interesting future research project might be for a historian to determine whether the spiralling demand for British manufactures in overseas markets in the late eighteenth century, with consumer attention to patterns, colours and well-produced fabrics, fed back into innovation by producers for this accelerating market. A start has recently been made on exploring these connections for the Yorkshire wool textile industry, where the growth of markets – notably in North America – and the new products that were manufactured in relation to consumer fashion clearly indicate that entrepreneurial energies focused as much on product design as on opportunities for sale. It became common for cloth to be made up according to intricate specifications based on the markets in which it was to be sold, with producers paying attention to new fibres, new colours and new patterns. By the 1790s the dyeing and finishing branches of the woollen trade, and to some extent the installation of carding engines and jennies in mills, were stimulated by the boom in cloth exports to North America (Smail, 1999).

The surge in exports in the final two decades of the eighteenth century appears to have made a positive impact on labour practices and the diffusion of technology in the British economy. If the labour force had produced mainly for the home market without the stimulus of expanding exports, lower levels of labour productivity would have been achieved because of prevailing unemployment, underemployment and cheap labour: it would not have been possible to reallocate the same labour inputs needed for export production just to cater for goods intended for the home market. In addition, the underuse of labour resources that resulted from the upper threshold of employment attainable in the home market meant that measured incomes would have been more modest without the stimulus of extra work made available by production for overseas markets (O'Brien and Engerman, 1991: 200–2; Engerman, 1996: 151). Total revenue from exports was increased by the growth of exports to British North America, generating additional jobs at home (Smith, 1995: 58–9). The argument here rests on the assumption that full alternative employment of labour resources would not have been possible in an economy in which underemployment was common among the labouring poor, though others might argue that greater specification of possible alternative uses for resources should be demonstrated (Engerman, 1998).

The rapid growth of cotton exports from mid-century onwards may have stimulated technological improvements on the spinning side of the industry by creating a larger market for finished cotton goods. If one discounts that statement by emphasising the prior importance of expanding domestic demand for cotton goods as the trigger for technological advance, the diffusion of the technical breakthrough accelerated during the export boom of the final twenty years of the century and was given greater impetus as a result. Those who regard the technological breakthrough in cotton spinning as a supply-side innovation have yet to demonstrate that it was not significantly related to market expansion, whether at home or abroad (Esteban, 1997: 899). In the thirty years after 1760 the timing of the rapid diffusion of cotton-spinning techniques via the spinning jenny, Arkwright's water frame and Crompton's mule appears to be closely linked to increased domestic and overseas demand – a growth in aggregate demand – for cotton fabrics. The larger overseas market for cotton clothing enlarged the total number of firms in the industry and aided competitiveness, while the need to compete with high-quality Indian cotton goods provided the impetus to cut costs, raise quality and instal new machinery to produce cotton checks and fustians (material with a linen warp and a cotton weft) for domestic and foreign markets (Crouzet, 1980: 92; Inikori, 1992).

At the turn of the nineteenth century, British industrial output was not circumscribed by home demand and the domestic market had also probably increased partly through productivity induced by overseas trade. Domestic demand served a larger market for goods and services than foreign demand but it was the latter that widened markets and gave greater scope for diffusing technical innovations to increase overall production in the British economy (Hudson, 1992: 199–200; Blackburn, 1997: 527). In other words, rising domestic demand, though an important feature of the flexibility and adaptability of business and labour in the economy, was not as important as foreign demand in promoting a dynamic, spiralling effect on marketing, innovation and industrial employment. It is possible to argue that the conditions of pre-industrial economies permitted only one nation to pioneer industrialisation (Hobsbawm, 1968: 48). If that was the case, integration of the export sector into an economy with increased manufacturing may well have been crucial in giving Britain a comparative advantage over other regions of western Europe poised for industrialisation by 1800 (though one must add the tapping of mineral resources, engineering skills and inventiveness to the list of advantages held by Britain's economy at that time).

6
Business institutions and the British economy

The development of commercial institutions was another important connection between Atlantic trade and eighteenth-century British economic development. Although these aspects of trade are not always quantifiable, they contributed much to the commercial dynamism of Britain. *Capitalism and Slavery* drew attention to the links between slave trading and the worlds of insurance and banking by pointing to the participation of the Liverpool slave trading families such as Heywood and Leyland in local banks, the recruitment of tobacco lords into the ranks of bankers in Glasgow and the emergence of the fire insurance companies from the ranks of London sugar refiners (E. Williams, 1944: 98–102, 104–5). More recent research has enabled us to identify more fully the connections between Atlantic trade and business developments, indicating the level of interpenetration between international trade, business institutions and the domestic economy; and it has provided enough material to emphasise the long-term benefits that this 'mix' of economic factors gave to British capitalism.

The financing of commerce

Several institutional improvements deserve mention. First of all, increased sophistication in the finance of commerce accompanied the growing scale and intricacy of Atlantic trade. An international payments mechanism involving bills of exchange enabled transfers to be made on either a bilateral or a multilateral basis between British, North American, West Indian and European port cities. This was particularly important since specie was often in short supply and commercial banks non-existent in British America. The use of bills of exchange usually involved four parties. It is best illustrated by a hypothetical example. A merchant in Philadelphia wishing to pay for export goods received from London would proceed as follows. Acting as a drawee (buyer), he would purchase a bill of exchange from a fellow Philadelphia businessman (the drawer or seller) who had a supply of them. The paper note was then sent to the London merchant who had dispatched the goods (the payee), who could submit it directly to a merchant, bill broker or bank (the payer). If the drawee endorsed the bill, he guaranteed to honour the amount written on it within the stated period. Thus a bill payable at ninety days' sight was one that could be cashed after three months. Once the bill had been endorsed it could be transferred from hand to hand as a negotiable instrument. After being cashed, the bill was returned to the original drawer to show that the sum specified had been paid. The system was something like using a modern cheque except that the financial instrument did not necessarily have to pass through a bank. If the bill was presented to a bank it could be discounted; but it was perfectly legal to circulate bills via the conduit of businessmen without using a bank. The latter practice had the advantage of increasing the money supply. The flexibility offered by bills of exchange was crucial both for the credit needs of eighteenth-century business and for the circulation of commodities in transatlantic trade (McCusker, 1978: 18–22; Neal, 1994: 157–60).

Bills of exchange were used extensively in the slave trade from about the 1670s onwards, when Barbadian planters established some agencies in London. Planters paid for slaves with such bills. Between 1672 and 1694 about 1,500 planters' bills worth almost £350,000 were remitted to the Royal African Company as payment for slave cargoes delivered (Sheridan, 1958: 253). Liverpool slave merchants in the eighteenth century had an extensive bill market in south Lancashire, with important London connections: a small number of acceptance houses in the metropolis served as payers of bills remitted to Liverpool for slave sales. This was the channel through which Liverpudlians realised their net profits easily and regularly; and it may be that this was a major reason for their success in the slave trade (Anderson, 1977). More generally, slavers trading with South Carolina and the Caribbean developed by the

1750s a system of remitting bills of exchange by insisting on payment 'in the bottom of the ship' that delivered the cargo, with specific times stated before interest became due. The terms of payment were usually either three, six, nine and twelve months or four, eight, twelve and sixteen months. This method of remittance was sometimes known as 'the guarantee system' because factors selling slaves had to name a surety to deal with their bills in Britain (Price, 1991: 311–17).

Marine insurance also benefited from the growth of war and international commerce; indeed, they were mutually reinforcing. The first corporate underwriters were the Royal Exchange Assurance and the London Assurance Company, both established in 1718 and the only two such enterprises permitted under the Bubble Act of 1720. These were supplemented by the chief private marine insurers at Lloyd's Coffee House, a great centre for decades for all aspects of shipping. The livelihood of underwriters at these three early centres of British marine insurance was closely linked to the higher premiums charged for hazardous long-distance voyages during eighteenth-century wars. Prompt news of the arrival and departure of ships and any losses at sea were of crucial importance to underwriters and insurance brokers, and so in 1734 Lloyd's List was established as a systematic way of dealing with the increasing volume of underwriting. It was supplemented from 1760 by Lloyd's Register of Shipping (Wright and Fayle, 1928; John, 1958; Supple, 1970). The best gains for insurance underwriters were made during wartime, with less charged for ships sailing with convoys. In peacetime premiums varied very little but higher rates were charged for return cargoes, because of the value of staple commodities in ships' holds. The hurricane season in the Caribbean during August and September and the possibility of high seas in the English Channel also pushed up insurance premiums on ships returning from the West Indies from the end of July to late January (Pares, 1936: 495–7; Crowhurst, 1977: 90, 94).

If marine insurance was stimulated by the growth of empire, so was fire insurance, which was important for the sugar refining industry. Refineries were often multi-storey wooden structures, employing expensive copper pans and copper and lead utensils. London had about 140 sugar refineries by 1776 and dominated the British industry. Similar concerns were found in Bristol, Liverpool,

Glasgow and Dublin. London sugar refiners helped to form the Phoenix Assurance Company in 1782. They were also involved with the Sun Fire Office (Trebilcock, 1985: 15–19, 56–9). A considerable amount of investment flowed into refineries. A case study of Bristol's sugar houses has shown that they attracted capital from merchants and other businessmen that amounted to about £60,000 in 1720 and £300,000 by 1760. Local refiners had accumulated sufficient profits to invest in a new fire insurance company, established in 1769 as the New Bristol Fire Office and set up partly to provide less expensive premiums than those charged by the major London fire insurance companies (K. Morgan, 1998: 149, 151). Marine and fire insurance both burgeoned in the eighteenth century; they were aided by the stimulus provided by an expanding Atlantic economy.

Atlantic trade also helped to foster a 'miniature banking revolution' in the outports. Between 1750 and 1775, colonial merchants became prominent partners in the first banks established in Bristol, Glasgow and Liverpool. The Ship Bank and the Glasgow Arms Bank (both established in 1752) and the Thistle Bank (1761), the first three banks founded in Glasgow, were all dominated by tobacco lords. Bristol's sugar, slave and tobacco merchants were among the founders of the Old Bank (1750), the Miles Bank (1752) and the Harford Bank (1769). One of the first local banks in Liverpool was Arthur Heywood Sons & Company, active in the slave trade. Liverpudlians trading with the Chesapeake also helped to form banks (Hyde, 1971: 18–19; Devine, 1975: 93–6; Price, 1980: 67–9, 94). This growth of banking in the provincial ports suited the needs of substantial businessmen by providing available deposit and transfer facilities. It also enabled large merchants in the outports who were partners in banks to tap the wealth of farmers, lesser traders and the urban professional classes through issuing bank notes, and hence to provide them with the necessary credit resources to carry on their own businesses. In this way, international trade made significant financial and business connections with the internal economy in Britain (Price, 1980: 67–8).

The provision of credit was a further way in which international trade was connected with more sophisticated financial transactions, so much so that one historian has referred to the existence of 'an empire of credit' (Bowen, 1996: 92). A substantial amount of credit was filtered into transatlantic commerce. For instance, on the eve of American independence around £4 million was extended by British merchants to American tobacco planters, and something like £9 million in credit was deployed in the west African–North American–Caribbean trading network (Price, 1980: 123). The chain of credit linked suppliers of goods in provincial Britain – staplers, packers, factors, warehousemen – with merchants at various British, American and West Indian ports and with stores and customers in North America and the Caribbean. In London's export trade with the Chesapeake, and probably in other branches of the export trade, the important intermediaries were large warehousemen, often linen drapers and ironmongers, who supplied goods on credit to export merchants and received credit from factors who had taken these wares from merchant-manufacturers, who in turn were supplied by cottage artisans. Credit was as important for Midlands manufacturers as for their textile counterparts in Yorkshire, Lancashire and Scotland (ibid.: 96–123). This web of credit transactions affected many commercial decisions in transatlantic trade and offered flexible options in payment for goods. The slave trade played a significant role in the deployment of credit over long distances. Credit was used in the Guinea traffic for purchasing East India goods and home-produced manufactures for exportation to the west African coast; for the sale of slaves in transatlantic areas; and for the sale of staple produce after the homeward-bound voyage (Inikori, 1990; Price, 1991: 299–323).

In the late eighteenth century, the length of commercial credit offered in the British export trade to North America was usually between six and twelve months. It expanded up to eighteen months in times of good trade but was reduced to less than six months when the business cycle experienced a downturn (K. Morgan, 2000a). Extension of credit could cause problems when goods were oversupplied to American markets and gluts resulted, as happened in the 1760s, early 1770s and mid-1780s when eager British exporters vended large bales of manufactured wares and extended credit even to smaller American importers and shopkeepers (Doerflinger, 1986: 88, 173–9, 266–7, 271; K. Morgan, 1993a: 112–15). But the large British export merchants were able to wait many months before payment was received: extending credit gave them access to a mobile factor of production and their reputation in trade helped to sustain many through short-term crises. Whatever the type of credit used, business dealings relied on the trust and obligation inherent in what was a highly personal way of transacting business (Zahedieh, 1998b; Mathias, 2000). Merchants beginning a correspondence with an overseas partner would enquire at the outset about the credit terms offered: this was perhaps the single most important piece of information needed to assess whether a business connection was worth pursuing. Despite the risks of extending credit, it is difficult to conceive of business enterprise in early modern Britain without the bedrock of widely available credit. And although credit was also embedded in transactions carried out in the domestic market, long-distance trade facilitated its use in a more sophisticated way.

Changing business strategies

Different branches of transatlantic trade evolved distinct forms of business organisation and marketing strategies that suited their geographical orientation plus demands created by their volume of shipping and commodity composition. The slave trade, because of its risky nature, was conducted by ad hoc partnerships that could change from voyage to voyage. In other words, businessmen invested in a particular voyage, though the managing agents often stayed in the trade for some time. Easy entry and exit of individuals from slave trading made the commerce very competitive (D. Richardson, 1976, 1985). In the early eighteenth century the tobacco trade was largely a consignment one, in which planters assumed title to the tobacco they shipped and used the services of British merchants as commission agents. A major change occurred after 1740, however, as Glasgow tobacco merchants sent out factors from the Clyde to run stores in the Chesapeake, purchase tobacco and market the leaf via a thriving re-export trade from Scotland to European markets. Under this system, entrepreneurial decisions were taken in the Chesapeake under a direct purchase system. Commission merchants at London and Bristol found it increasingly difficult to get consignments from planters so after 1763 they developed a 'cargo' trade with independent Chesapeake merchants whom they supplied with exports on their own account (Price,

1954; 1980: 127–8; Devine, 1975; Devine and Jackson, 1995: 146–50). The sugar trade also relied to some extent on direct purchase of sugar on the spot in the West Indies, but under pressure from London merchants it became increasingly a commission trade in which planters retained ownership of the crop and shipped it on commission to factors in British ports, who sold it to refineries (Davies, 1952; Pares, 1960: 33–4, 47–8; Sheridan, 1973: 319–38; K. Morgan, 1993a: 193–8). These different business techniques helped merchants to consolidate their business expertise in an increasingly complex Atlantic economy in the eighteenth century.

New commercial strategies employed during the post-1783 export boom were another business development associated with long-distance trade as merchants on both sides of the Atlantic learned to shift rapidly between various markets for their goods. A number of American merchants, notably Quakers, toured Britain to investigate industrial developments and internal improvements and to find out about goods and prices, credit terms offered, commission and brokerage charges, and other business information, with a view to better judgement of their commercial connections with British merchants. One such traveller, the Philadelphian Jabez Fisher, left a detailed notebook with assessments of the credit standing of inland and port merchants throughout Britain at the time of the American Revolution – an indication of the importance of gathering accurate information on the credit-worthiness of potential correspondents (K. Morgan, 1992, 2000a).

After 1790 British woollen manufacturers often sent out agents or partners to the United States, something which helped to quicken the pace of sales and to provide closer supervision of the composition of woollen shipments for different markets. At the same time close links were forged between American merchants and British businessmen, with personnel sent to and fro across the Atlantic to gain knowledge of the varied export wares on offer and to see, on the spot, the best ways of gauging price and quality in relation to diverse consumer tastes. The shift towards more aggressive marketing strategies has been examined for trade in the 1780s between British ports and Philadelphia, the largest city and the biggest port in the new United States. Instead of allowing their American correspondents to assume title to the goods they exported, many British firms began to ship off large cargoes on their own account, and often dispatched young partners to Philadelphia to solicit business. Moreover some British adventurers purchased goods on credit, took them to Philadelphia, rented a store and sold the goods on their own account (Doerflinger, 1986: 245).

In addition, a number of merchants left Britain for substantial periods of time to conduct business in North America and some Americans came to British ports to set up in trade. Scottish factors in the Chesapeake, keeping well-stocked supplies of dry goods throughout the tobacco-growing areas, are among the best-known of these migrants; they flourished from the 1740s onwards. But one also finds a cosmopolitan element of British merchants in Philadelphia, New York, Baltimore, Charleston and Boston, and Americans settling at Bristol, Liverpool and London. While these migrants criss-crossing the Atlantic were a minority of merchants in specific ports, they took with them knowledge of the range of goods best suited for shipment across the ocean (K. Morgan, 2000a). Innovations in business practice and the mobility made feasible by transatlantic shipping routes were a response by merchants to widening economic opportunities, increased competition and the risk environment of oceanic trading – though the obverse of this situation was that textiles and trade were the most prominent sectors of the economy for English bankrupts during early industrialisation (Hoppit, 1987).

The size of merchant firms

The growth and complexity of Atlantic trade led to another significant business development, namely, an increase in the size and style of British merchant houses. Between 1675 and 1775 – and especially in the latter half of that period – there was a considerable increase in the concentration of tobacco and sugar imports among large firms in Bristol and Glasgow, and a squeezing out of marginal competitors; and this also occurred to a lesser degree in London and Liverpool. Thus, for instance, over 200 firms imported tobacco at Bristol in 1702; after mid-century, the number was always less than thirty and sometimes amounted to single figures. In the sugar trade at Bristol over 500 importers could be found by the late 1720s; this number was consistently whittled down, and by the end of the century Bristol had 85 sugar importers. London had 573 firms importing tobacco in 1676, 117 in 1719 and 56 in 1775. By the 1780s and 1790s, a similar concentration was apparent among slave traders at London, Liverpool and Bristol. To take Bristol as an example once more, just two merchants owned almost 40 per cent of the tonnage of African vessels clearing from the port in 1789–91 (Price and Clemens, 1987; Inikori, 1990; K. Morgan, 1993a: 143, 158–60, 189, 191–2).

The increase in concentration ratios points to a considerable 'revolution of scale' in the conduct of some major branches of transatlantic trade. It was assisted by the availability of marine insurance and credit to large, seemingly secure firms. This transformation of the size and style of firms led to higher levels of capitalisation and to greater economic efficiency in the conduct of business, with large turnovers of goods speeded up by the concentration of resources. Whether a similar trend occurred in the export trades is virtually impossible to determine given the great variety of manufactured wares dispatched overseas and the lack of an obvious way of ranking merchants from records which neither total the value of exporters' cargoes nor provide consistent weights and measures susceptible to tabulation. Yet in the mid-eighteenth century export trade from Britain to Philadelphia, the same large London merchant firms appear again and again, suggesting impressionistically that concentration may also have been increasingly common among exporters (Doerflinger, 1986: 87).

The circulation of business information

Atlantic trade gave impetus to the circulation of business information in various settings. After 1660 most ports had coffee houses where merchants met to discuss shipping and trade; some London coffee houses specialised in catering for West India, Virginia or Carolina merchants. Newspapers flourished in London, throughout provincial Britain and in the North American ports in the eighteenth century; they grew in number as the century progressed. By the era of the American Revolution, both Bristol and Philadelphia, two thriving port cities in the British Empire, had several weekly newspapers. There were fewer newspapers in the Caribbean but they were published regularly in Jamaica. Many newspapers carried details on shipping news, giving dates of arrival and departure and the destinations of vessels. Those in North American ports, such as the *Pennsylvania Gazette* and the *Virginia Gazette*, provided detailed information on imported slaves and British goods. Advertisements in such sources often included full details of the commodities for sale at colonial wharves and quays.

These details could be supplemented by several other outlets for printed commercial information: Lloyd's Shipping List and Lloyd's Register, described above; marine lists publishing details about the arrival and departure of ships at various ports; printed bills of entry listing commodities imported and exported at a given port of entry; commodity price currents, which published lists of goods and their wholesale selling prices; exchange rate currents, which gave the rates at which foreign bills of exchange sold locally; and the transatlantic postal system operating via packet boats from Falmouth across the Atlantic (Steele, 1986; McCusker, 1997: 145–76). During the eighteenth century, merchants disseminated a more varied range of samples and business documents, which added to the accuracy of commercial information that was circulated. In the British export trade to North America there was, for instance, a marked trend towards sending correspondents pattern books of manufacturers' goods, samples of textiles, printed sheets with prices and ranges of commodities and printed partnership papers when a new firm was established or when partners changed (K. Morgan, 2000a). A higher volume of commercial information was transmitted more rapidly as the eighteenth century progressed, with ever more precise details about maritime affairs, which helped to foster more accurate business judgements. The improvement in business communication has aptly been seen as creating 'a consolidated English Atlantic' (Steele, 1986: 276).

7

Atlantic trade and British ports

As *Capitalism and Slavery* suggested, and as modern research has confirmed, Atlantic trade was crucial for the development of Britain's west coast outports and had a significant impact on the metropolis (E. Williams, 1944: 60–4, 73–5). Virtually all ports around Britain participated in transatlantic commerce to some degree. On England's south coast Plymouth, Poole, Southampton and Cowes served as customs points for goods from the Americas intended for re-export markets in Europe. Bideford, Barnstaple and several other small Devon ports imported tobacco down to the mid-eighteenth century (Price, 1973, vol. I: 590–4; 1996b; Jackson, 1983: 190–1). Lancaster developed a minor role in the slave trade that stimulated its economic development (Elder, 1992). Even ports on the east coast of Britain, such as Hull and Newcastle upon Tyne, had a smattering of merchants who conducted transatlantic voyages. Yet all these ports engaged in such traffic on a relatively small scale: they lacked the demographic growth, geographical location, processing industries or industrialising hinterland neces-sary to stimulate Atlantic trade and shipping on a large scale. By 1775 the smaller ports, such as Falmouth and Lancaster, had largely dropped out of transatlantic trade as it became more complex, specialised and subject to economies of scale. The larger ports that flourished in long-distance commerce were maritime centres where transaction costs could be kept low. One might wonder why ports on the south coast of England did not play a larger role in the Atlantic economy given the easy access of the English Channel to the Bay of Biscay and then the ocean. The answer is that the re-export trade of such ports – Southampton, Portsmouth, Poole – was often left unprotected in the war years

from 1689 to 1713 and was affected again by enemy privateering in later years of conflict during the eighteenth century (Price, 1998: 92–3).

The west coast outports

The main outports stimulated by the growth of eighteenth-century Atlantic trade were naturally those with a westward outlook: Bristol, Liverpool, Whitehaven (on the Cumberland coast) and Glasgow. In 1700 Bristol was the largest of the four, both in population size and in the volume and value of its trading activities, but by 1800 Liverpool and Glasgow had mounted a firm challenge to Bristol's position. Whitehaven, as we shall see, was the least significant of these participants in transatlantic trade. During the course of the eighteenth century, each of the three leading west coast outports specialised more and more in a particular line of transatlantic trade: Glasgow in the tobacco trade, Liverpool in the slave trade, Bristol in the sugar trade (Price, 1954: 190). Though each port had a much wider range of commerce than this summary implies, nevertheless these were three of the largest trades across the Atlantic. A brief consideration of why these ports diverged over time in the main focus of their Atlantic trading activities will help to pinpoint how such commerce affected port cities and their hinterlands and thus how different patterns of trade and business organisation made an impact on the British economy.

Whitehaven was briefly prominent in the tobacco trade in the 1740s, when interruption of sea lanes by French privateers in the mouth of the English Channel during wartime made it prudent to ship Chesapeake tobacco around the north of Ireland. But it eventually reverted to concentration on the coal trade (tapping the mineral resources of Cumberland) to coastwise areas and Ireland. Whitehaven had a limited interest in the sugar and slave trades, and it sustained only a small merchant community: in 1743, when Whitehaven's tobacco imports were second only to London, only twenty-one men were directly involved in that trade. Whitehaven's short-lived role in Atlantic trade was mainly confined to the tobacco trade in the 1730s and 1740s. It re-exported most of the tobacco it received. Isolated from much of the rest of Britain, Whitehaven merchants had to assemble export cargoes from considerable distances because the port's hinterland was sparsely populated and local goods produced (such as coal) were unsuitable for long-distance trade. In addition, Whitehaven encountered difficulty in establishing import-processing manufactures. As J. V. Beckett notes, west Cumberland 'was hampered in its development by a small market and a slowly increasing population; hence it was unable to establish consumer goods industries which could compete in the overseas, or even the national market'. To compound these problems, Whitehaven had neither a natural haven nor a suitable site on a river (Price, 1973, vol. I: 590, 594–604; Corfield, 1982: 43; Beckett, 1981: xii, 104, 106–8, 112, 119–20, 142–6, 155 (quotation), 156).

Glasgow's population was only 14,000 in 1660 but it had risen to 77,000 by 1801, with rapid development particularly in the last two decades of the eighteenth century (Devine and Jackson, 1995: 63, 122). Glasgow rose from being a small port in 1700 to become one of the great commercial cities of eighteenth-century Europe; and this was achieved largely by generating new marketing strategies and productivity advances in tobacco shipment. From the early eighteenth century, but especially from the 1740s, Glaswegians sent out factors to run stores in the Chesapeake and got them to supply not only a wide range of British consumer goods to American customers but to adopt the direct purchase of tobacco as opposed to the consignment trade in that staple crop. By the 1770s there were also Scottish firms operating independent merchant houses and wholesale businesses in Virginia and Maryland. Concentrating largely on oronoco tobacco – darker and more in mass demand than the sweet-scented variety – they also pioneered an effective marketing strategy that enabled them to re-export the tobacco crop in bulk from the Clyde to the French farmers-general and to the Netherlands and Germany. By the end of the Seven Years War Glasgow was beginning to challenge London's leadership in the Anglo-American tobacco trade, and by the early 1770s it had assumed the premier position among British ports in the trade. Taking advantage of Scottish laws, Glasgow merchants formed large, interlocking partnerships, giving them better access to capital and credit resources. By carrying the most valuable staple product grown in North America to continental European markets, Glasgow produced dynasties of tobacco lords that laid the economic foundations for the growth of trading activity on the Clyde (Price, 1954; 1973, vol. I: 588–93, 604–17; Devine, 1975; Devine and Jackson, 1995: 139–83).

Without tobacco, Glasgow would not have reached eminence as a commercial city. Unlike Bristol and Liverpool, Glasgow had the initial disadvantage of not having an urban economy capable of sustaining the flow of imported commodities before 1750. The establishment of two outports, Port Glasgow and Greenock, provided local facilities to cope with the growing volume and diversity of trade at a time when it was still not feasible to dredge the barely navigable river Clyde. The entrepôt trade provided by tobacco from the Chesapeake 'was the fastest way of creating mercantile wealth on a meagre economic base' (Devine and Jackson, 1995: 77). It was supplemented by a small West India trade before the American Revolution that burgeoned after 1783, with Glasgow's sugar imports being exceeded only by those of London, Bristol and Liverpool by the 1790s. Glaswegians hardly participated directly in the slave trade, though there were plenty of Scots factors in the Caribbean who had a direct or indirect involvement in that nefarious commerce (Devine, 1978; K. Morgan, 1993a: 188, 190).

After 1750 merchant finance flowed from Glasgow's tobacco lords into industry and shipping services connected with the port and into its banks and manufacturing sector. A partnership between trade and manufacturing was sustained at Glasgow from the late seventeenth century to the mid-nineteenth century, with trade sometimes gaining the ascendancy over industry and sometimes vice versa, but with both intertwining to promote the city's economic development and transition to industrialisation. Glasgow had no urban rival in the west of Scotland. It also benefited from expanding industrial activities in its region in the late eighteenth and early nineteenth centuries in cotton, iron, shipbuilding and coal-mining. By 1830 the port and its manufacturing enterprises comprised the one major British port and city where industrial development and trade took place in one urban space. As T. M. Devine has succinctly put it, 'Glasgow combined the functions of great ports such as Liverpool and leading industrial centres like Manchester in one urban entity' (Devine, 1977; Devine and Jackson, 1995: 14 (quotation), 235).

Liverpool prospered by the growth of oceanic trade to become the most important slave trading port in the world by 1800. Between 1699 and 1807, the period when the British slave trade was open to private merchant firms, it dispatched 5,199 slaving vessels out of a total of 12,103 clearances from British ports, and easily exceeded the number of Guinea vessels sailing from Bristol and London (D. Richardson, 1998: 446; cf. D. Richardson, 1989b: 184–95). Liverpool also participated in other major lines of transatlantic trade. It assumed second place among British ports in the tobacco trade by 1738, a position lost to Glasgow in the generations before 1776 but then regained by the mid-1790s. Liverpool was the third sugar-importing centre in Britain, after London and Bristol, for most of the eighteenth century, but in the late 1790s it overtook the 'metropolis of the west' (Price and Clemens, 1987: 39–40; K. Morgan, 1993a: 154, 188–90). Unlike Bristol, where tobacco and sugar merchants were distinct groups with very little overlap of personnel, Liverpool benefited from merchants who dealt as readily in sugar as tobacco (Clemens, 1976: 219). This probably enabled Liverpudlians to switch their main focus in Atlantic trade more easily than at Bristol, and thus to respond more quickly to shifts in market conditions caused by war, financial crises and changing patterns of demand.

Liverpool also experienced diversified demographic and commercial growth in the first half of the eighteenth century. This altered the city from a 'small yet energetic port' to 'a major urban-commercial centre' (Clemens, 1976: 216–22). The population of the city was about 4,000 in 1680, rising to 34,000 in 1773 and 83,000 in 1801, placing it second among English provincial towns (after Manchester and Salford together). Such growth gave the opportunity for its merchants to exploit the trading possibilities of the Anglo-American market (Corfield, 1982: 15, 183). The increase in the volume of Liverpool's trade was sustained after 1720 by the construction of five wet and two dry docks, which protected ships against damage and allowed for more efficient loading and un-loading of cargoes (Hyde, 1971: 10–15, 31–4, 72–7; Clemens, 1976). Liverpool's shipping had geographical advantages in wartime, lying out of reach of most enemy privateers because ships could sail north of Ireland. Merchants at the port could tap the linen and cotton industries of south Lancashire. This was an increasingly important consideration given that textiles were always the main commodities marketed for slaves with African traders and Liverpool, of all British slave trading ports, was the one most successful in substituting homespun textiles for imported East Indian fabrics in the late eighteenth century. Liverpool was well placed to take advantage of smuggled East India goods intended for the slave trade and lodged in the Isle of Man, which lay beyond the normal British customs jurisdiction. The port's advantage in transatlantic slaving also came from Liverpudlians' business acumen in searching out new markets for slaves and handling bills of exchange in a way that tapped the south Lancashire capital market as well as financial connections with London (Ramsay, 1957: 151–65; Anderson, 1977; D. Richardson, 1976; Price, 1996b: 30–1).

An extensive hinterland developed around Liverpool. The cotton industry in south Lancashire lay within the orbit of the port and significant business links were forged between Liverpool merchants and Manchester manufacturers. After 1770 good canal links between the Mersey, the industrial North West and the Midlands facilitated the flow of export goods into the port of Liverpool. By 1800 Liverpool was better connected to an inland network of communications than any British port of comparable size. The Leeds and Liverpool and Trent and Mersey canals linked up with the Mersey estuary. They were the arteries through which raw materials were channelled efficiently from the dockside to the cotton mills and along which manufactured textiles were sent in the opposite direction. Liverpool's striking commercial growth in the late eighteenth century thus combined success as an Atlantic entrepôt with the rapid development of industry and transport in its hinterland: home demand and foreign demand intertwined there as a result (Langton, 1983). These dual developments provided the platform for Liverpool's important role in the nineteenth-century Atlantic economy, especially its participation in the cotton trade and shipping lines (Hyde, 1971).

At Bristol, merchants profited from broadly based Atlantic commercial interests. Bristol participated in the slave, tobacco and sugar trades to a significant extent, and also exported many goods to the colonies. Some of these drew upon its own industries, such as glassmaking and copper- and brassware. But an extensive hinterland, with rapid economic and demographic growth, did not develop around Bristol during the eighteenth century even though the city's population grew from 20,000 in 1700 to 64,000 in 1801. And Bristol lost ground to its main outport rivals in both the tobacco and slave trades largely because of more business acumen at Liverpool and Glasgow. Bristol was passed in the level of tobacco imports by its main provincial rivals in the first half of the eighteenth century – by Glasgow in the 1720s, by Liverpool in 1738 and by Whitehaven in 1739. Although Bristol always had a significant commitment to the slave trade, it was overtaken by Liverpool in the 1740s. Bristol's share of the total tonnage engaged in the British slave trade plummeted from 42 per cent in 1738–42 to 24 per cent in 1753–7 to 10 per cent in 1773–7 and to a mere 1 per cent in 1803–7 (Price and Clemens, 1987: 39–40; D. Richardson, 1989b: 185–95). Bristol never recovered its position in these trades once it had been overtaken by other outports.

Continuing influxes of sugar by a cohesive mercantile elite helped to moderate Bristol's relative commercial decline by keeping up the value of commodities entering the port. Bristol imported almost 21,000 hogsheads of sugar in 1773, making it the leading British outport in the trade. Sugar was processed in the city's sugar refineries. In 1781 Bristol's gross customs receipts comprised £243,370, just ahead of Liverpool, the second outport, with £241,587, and this was made possible partly by influxes of sugar and other imports of relatively high value. Liverpool began to challenge Bristol's position in the sugar trade only in 1799 and 1800 (K. Morgan, 1993a: 189–90; 1993b; 1998). Bristol's commitment to sugar importing became greater as the eighteenth century progressed. It represented something of a paradox. In some ways it made perfect commercial sense: sugar was the most valuable imported commodity to Britain; it was the one import trade regularly protected by fleets and convoys in wartime before the Napoleonic wars; and refined sugar could be re-exported, sent coastwise or distributed throughout South West England on a significant scale.

Yet concentration on sugar also had drawbacks. By having its trade and industry so geared towards imports, and specifically sugar, Bristol developed as more of a consumption centre than as an entrepôt for foreign trade, like Liverpool and Glasgow, with a surplus of mass-produced industrial goods for export. Bristol remained relatively insignificant as an export centre throughout its modern history, ranking fifteenth among British ports for exports in 1857 (K. Morgan, 1996b: 59). Specialisation in sugar helped to boost sugar refineries, rum distilling, brewing and cocoa and chocolate manufacture but probably retarded growth in other sectors of the urban economy. A consumption centre based around processing of tropical produce and distributing trades failed to generate significant multiplier or spread effects. It did not stimulate the structural economic change found at other ports concerned with a growing volume of exports to world-wide markets, ports that tapped expanding demographic and industrial urban centres and hinterlands based on higher rates and younger ages of marriage, rising wage labour and productivity gains in industry (K. Morgan, 1993a: 222–3; 1996b: 63). Bristol was also slow to expand its port facilities during the eighteenth century. The Society of Merchant Venturers, which leased the quays from the city of Bristol, made improvements to the quays and wharves, but congestion in the centre of the port was only partially solved, after much procrastination, with the building of a floating harbour between 1804 and 1809 (K. Morgan, 1993a: 31–2).

The port of London

London's population grew from c. 575,000 in 1700 to 959,000 by 1801, making it the largest city in western Europe and one of the biggest in the world. Its sheer size meant that it was always a large market for the products of colonial trade and for distribution and re-export. Already by the late seventeenth century transatlantic trade provided an important quantitative and qualitative stimulus to London's economy: in 1686 the colonies shipped goods worth over £1 million to London, enabling customers there to purchase manufactured goods from the proceeds. Transatlantic commerce initially attracted a large number of merchants in the metropolis but was soon dominated by a relatively small group (Zahedieh, 1994: 259; 1999: 146–8). About a quarter of the capital's workforce was apparently employed in trades connected with the port. London had many consumer-oriented industries derived from the wealth produced by overseas trade and government expenditure: these included textile finishing and sugar refining. Its merchants co-ordinated people, products and capital and thereby helped to integrate the economy of the British Empire (French, 1992; Cain and Hopkins, 1993: 62; Hancock, 1995). The merchant community of London was cosmopolitan; the financial hub of the metropolis attracted continental traders including Dutch, Huguenots, Germans and Jews, who all participated in the capital's commerce with its American hinterlands (Jones, 1988: 254–60; Ormrod, 1993; Bowen, 1996: 150–2). By the mid-eighteenth century, London was an international mercantile centre; over three-quarters of the firms listed in Mortimer's *Universal Director* (1763) included partners of foreign extraction (Chapman, 1992: 23, 30).

A large proportion of the nation's trade always flowed in and out of the capital city. But the relative share of London's commercial dominance declined during the eighteenth century. At the beginning of the century London took 80 per cent of the imports entering England, 65 per cent of the exports and 85 per cent of the re-exports. By 1772–4, these shares had been cut back by the rise of the outports to 72 per cent of imports, 62 per cent of exports and 72 per cent of re-exports. London's relatively declining share of commodity trade in the eighteenth century was counterbalanced by a greater rate of growth at the outports: between 1700 and 1776 imports at the outports increased more than twice as rapidly as London's and re-exports grew three times as quickly (French, 1992: 28–9). Operating deficiencies at the port of London played their part in the capital's declining share of overseas trade in the eighteenth century. There was an increase in the number of wharves and quays in the port of London in the 1670s and 1680s but no commercial docks were constructed on the River Thames until the turn of the nineteenth century. The legal quays, where alone dutiable goods could be shipped, were very congested; no single authority had control over the port of London; and there were frequent disputes between wharfingers, operating after 1695 as a secret cartel, and their merchant-clients, including a good many sugar and tobacco merchants. Lighters had to be used for unloading vessels in midstream or down river, and this led to delays, easier theft of goods and extra expense for merchants. The Corporation of the City of London resisted plans for port reform. The metropolis failed to provide adequate dock facilities for its vast array of ships and cargoes until just after 1800 (Roseveare, 1996, 2000).

Despite these internal port problems, London still dominated British overseas trade by the time of the American Revolution and had a large shipping industry, a broadly based merchant community and a number of important commercial and financial institutions – the Lombard and West End Banks, the Bank of England, Lloyd's Coffee House, the Royal Exchange and so on. These enabled London's business community to garner extensive earnings from insurance, trade credits, freights and warehousing (Corfield, 1982: 72–3; Daunton, 1995: 372, 542). London's vast emporium of goods and its financial servicing also aided the Atlantic trade of the outports in significant ways. As the headquarters of the English East India Company, London supplied Asian textiles and cowrie shells to Liverpool slave traders; they also handled sugar and other commodities sent back to Britain to cover the bills of slave sales. London remained an important centre for finance of the slave trade throughout the eighteenth century (D. Richardson, 1998: 449). By 1750 many London merchants were acting as commission agents, bankers and insurers for provincial ports, paying the proceeds owed by foreign merchants to British manufacturers (Chapman, 1992: 61–2). In terms of the volume of shipping and value of the cargoes it handled, as well as its financial institutions, thriving merchant community and consumer industries, London's economic development was boosted significantly by foreign trade.

Conclusion

Throughout this book the suggested links between the slave–sugar complex, Atlantic trade and the British economy have been delineated for the period 1660–1800, with particular reference to the issues raised in Eric Williams's *Capitalism and Slavery*, subsequent scholarship debating matters discussed therein and the various positions taken by historians looking at the interplay of home demand and foreign demand in British economic development. In the seventeenth and eighteenth centuries Britain had a thriving transatlantic trade, both on a bilateral and a multilateral basis, which grew over time. Receiving protection from privateers and the navy during frequent years of war, British trade coped with interruptions to normal shipping lanes probably better than its chief maritime rivals, the French. The pursuit of trade was aided by the revenues collected by the state that underpinned overseas expansion. Mercantilism, far from being a yoke that Britain needed to discard, proved a successful means of running a grand marine empire: shipping and trade, supported by naval strength, progressed over the long term despite temporary setbacks in times of commercial depression or war. Colonies were established in both North America and the West Indies, and trading posts maintained throughout the Atlantic trading world. The slave trade and slavery were central to the settler societies established in the New World and to the production of staple crops for European consumption. They provided a specific type of labour (enforced bondage based on racial discrimination) on a particular type of agricultural complex (the plantation) that produced profits for investors tied to the mother country. A great deal of wealth was generated in Atlantic trade and American plantations by merchants and planters in particular, but the means by which this was funnelled back to Britain were complex.

Detailed research into slavery and the slave trade have led to a more sophisticated approach to the gains from slavery and the slave trade than was once common. Advances in quantitative techniques and extra primary material gathered since the time when Eric Williams was writing suggest that it is no longer accurate to state that the profits of the slave trade were consistently high: annual net returns in the trade were relatively modest because of the need to offset victualling and transport costs and the sheer risk involved in voyages touching at three continents and lasting for more than a calendar year. Calculations of the ratio of slave trading profits to commercial and industrial investment have shown that the *potential* contribution could have been quite high, but empirical studies of slave merchants and their investments have not proven that this was the case. Plenty of capital was amassed from slave plantations in the West Indian islands, which were the most valuable possessions in the eighteenth-century British Empire.

Despite the lucrative private returns arising from these investments, however, the various arguments for slavery and sugar's role in metropolitan capital accumulation have not proven that the direct connection between the two was substantial. The matter needs further examination. More thorough wealth estimates of the British Caribbean are needed, especially for the period after the American Revolution. Firmer evidence needs to be adduced on the extent to which West India fortunes were repatriated, given that liquidity – with much capital tied up in mortgages, annuities, bonds and plantation debts – was by no means an automatic option. And better analysis of the multiplier effects created by colonial capital in Britain are also needed. The economic health of the British Caribbean, *pace* Ragatz and Williams, was buoyant by the late eighteenth century, but the private fortunes made from sugar did not lead to industrial investment in Britain on the whole. It could be argued that the propensity of West India merchants and planters to channel funds into conspicuous consumption boosted British economic development in so far as building country houses and laying out landscape gardens stimulated the construction industry and one important aspect of agricultural improvement; but it is doubtful whether the impetus was on a sufficient financial scale to have had a major impact. The extent to which the colonies were a net gain or net loss to Britain has not been proven definitively, partly because of difficulties in estimating the income and expenditure involved; and so we are still not able to state with accuracy whether Adam Smith's view of the colonies as a drain on British resources was justified.

Nevertheless, even if the direct contribution of capital amassed in the slave trade, slavery and other transatlantic ventures to metropolitan economic growth is still much debated, there were significant links between Atlantic trade and eighteenth-century British economic development. The intricate connections between consumer demand and British exports, aided by population growth in the Americas and income from the slave–sugar nexus, helped to boost and vary manufactured exports at a time when transatlantic markets were capturing an increasing portion of British overseas trade. Without the stimulus of American and West Indian demand for linens, cottons, metalware and hardware – added to the domestic demand for such wares – it is unlikely that those industries would have increased their production capacity to the degree that occurred in the quarter-century before the American Revolution. Though we need better data on the proportion of goods manufactured in specific industries that was exported, new evidence has shown that the share of industrial exports in industrial production was rising on trend from the early eighteenth until the mid-nineteenth century; and that over half the incremental ratio of industrial production was exported during the two decades at the end of the eighteenth century when an acceleration into an industrialising economy is evident in estimates of British economic growth. A strong case can be made for greater production of manufactures in late eighteenth-century Britain as a result of the additional demand created by American and Caribbean markets. Possibly this growth in aggregate demand induced technical diffusion, greater employment and better productivity among industrial communities in and around British ports and their hinterlands.

The growth of business institutions such as long-term credit, banks and marine and fire insurance, as well as greater and more accurate circulation of business information, was important for the long-term development of the British economy, improving commercial and financial expertise and services. It would be legitimate to see such business developments as derivative from the growth of long-distance trade, shipping and mercantile endeavour, but this does not diminish their significance. Atlantic trade also had a considerable impact on shipping and ports and their hinterlands. London's trade and shipping thrived partly because of the opportunities provided by transatlantic ventures. Despite problems with the efficiency of the eighteenth-century port of London, the metropolis still served as the hub of many avenues of commerce and as a leading financial emporium. West coast outports such as Bristol, Liverpool and Glasgow also benefited from Atlantic commercial activities. In the case of Liverpool and Glasgow, the growth of transatlantic trade in the eighteenth century was accompanied by substantial demographic and industrial development. They combined industrial and commercial development in one urban centre in areas where manufacturing production was increasing and where, as a result, home demand and foreign demand could be combined successfully within a region.

Foreign commerce provided work for merchants, shipowners, shipbuilders, customs officials, packers, hauliers, dock labourers, seamen, nautical instrument makers and workers in the royal dockyards. Less tangibly, it stimulated the development of commercial education (as at Warrington Academy), entrepreneurship and attitudes towards accumulation and investment (Price, 1980; Minchinton, 1969: 45–8; Mathias, 1983: 96). All these aspects of the economy have to be considered when looking at the contribution of slavery and Atlantic trade to the eighteenth-century British economy; to concentrate just on the direct impact of trade on manufacturing industry nationally is too narrow a focus (Hudson, 1992: 189). Moreover, to gauge the performance of trade in relation to national income is bound to understate the significance of the external contribution to economic change because it tells us nothing about the dynamic, spiralling impact of commerce on an industrialising economy. On the contrary, it is the methodological approach most likely to minimise the role of the external sector in relation to growth.

Slavery and Atlantic trade made an important, though not decisive, impact on Britain's long-term economic development between the late Stuart era and the early Victorian age, playing their part in enabling Britain to become the workshop of the world (O'Brien and Escosura, 1998: 58–9). The ever increasing scholarship on these matters now accords a positive role to the connections between slavery, trade, empire and a British economy experiencing the transition to industrialisation, even though it still recognises the significance of endogenous factors leading to economic change. *Capitalism and Slavery* raised hypotheses related to many of these themes without analysing them fully; yet it deserves credit as a pioneering, influential study. My own emphasis on increasing commercial sophistication, flexibility and efficiency in the British Atlantic economy underlines the burden of this book: that transatlantic trade and slavery were indeed significant for British economic development between 1660 and 1800, especially after 1750, but as much for their stimulus to manufacturing production in textiles, metalware and hardware, receipts from the sale of invisibles, financial intermediation and business improvements as for their direct impact on capital investment and national income.

Bibliography

The place of publication is London unless otherwise indicated.

Anderson, B. L. (1977) 'The Lancashire Bill System and Its Liverpool Practitioners: The Case of a Slave Merchant' in W. H. Chaloner and B. M. Ratcliffe (eds.) *Trade and Transport: Essays in Economic History in Honour of T. S. Willan.* Manchester.

Anderson, B. L. and Richardson, David (1983) 'Market Structure and Profits of the British African Trade in the Late Eighteenth Century: A Comment', *Journal of Economic History*, 43, 713–21.

(1985) 'Market Structure and the Profits of the British African Trade in the Late Eighteenth Century: A Rejoinder Rebutted', *Journal of Economic History*, 45, 705–7.

Anstey, R. (1968) 'Capitalism and Slavery: A Critique', *Economic History Review*, 2nd ser., 21, 307–20.

(1975a) *The Atlantic Slave Trade and British Abolition 1760–1810.* A major assessment of British slaving activity and the early abolitionist movement.

(1975b) 'The Volume and Profitability of the British Slave Trade, 1761–1807' in S. L. Engerman and E. D. Genovese (eds.) *Race and Slavery in the Western Hemisphere: Quantitative Studies.* Princeton, N.J.

(1976) 'The British Slave Trade, 1761–1807: A Comment', *Journal of African History*, 17, 606–7.

Aufhauser, R. K. (1974) 'Profitability of Slavery in the British Caribbean', *Journal of Interdisciplinary History*, 5, 45–67.

Bailey, R. W. (1986) 'Africa, the Slave Trade and the Rise of Industrial Capitalism in Europe and the United States', *American History: A Bibliographic Review*, 2, 1–91.

Bairoch, P. (1973) 'Commerce international et genèse de la révolution industrielle anglaise', *Annales ESC*, 28, 541–71.

Baugh, D. A. (1994) 'Maritime Strength and Atlantic Commerce: The Uses of a "Grand Marine Empire"' in L. Stone (ed.) *An Imperial State at War: Britain from 1689 to 1815.*

Bean, R. N. (1975) *The British Trans-Atlantic Slave Trade, 1650–1775.* New York.

Beckett, J. V. (1981) *Coal and Tobacco: The Lowthers and the Economic Development of West Cumberland, 1660–1760.* Cambridge.

Beckles, H. (1982) 'Down But Not Out: Eric Williams' *Capitalism and Slavery* After Nearly Forty Years of Criticism', *Bulletin of Eastern Caribbean Affairs,* 8, 29–36.

(1984) 'Capitalism and Slavery: The Debate over the Williams Thesis', *Social and Economic Studies,* 33, 171–90.

(1987) ' "The Williams Effect": Eric Williams's *Capitalism and Slavery* and the Growth of West Indian Political Economy' in Solow and Engerman (1987).

(1998) 'Capitalism, Slavery and Caribbean Modernity', *Callaloo,* 20, 777–89. This appears in an issue of a journal that includes a helpful bibliography of works by and about Eric Williams.

(1999)'Economic Interpretations of Caribbean history' in B. W. Higman (ed.) *General History of the Caribbean, vol. 6: Methodology and Historiography.*

Behrendt, S. D. (1993) 'The British Slave Trade, 1785–1807: Volume, Profitability, and Mortality', University of Wisconsin Ph.D. The most thorough study of quantitative aspects of the last phase of the British slave trade.

Berg, M. (1994) *The Age of Manufactures, 1700–1820,* 2nd edn.

Berrill, K. (1960) 'International Trade and the Rate of Economic Growth', *Economic History Review,* 2nd ser., 12, 351–9.

Blackburn, R. (1997) *The Making of New World Slavery: From the Baroque to the Modern 1492–1800.* A recent left-wing appraisal of slavery's role in the making of the modern world.

Blaut, J. M. (1993) *The Colonizers' Model of the World: Geographical Diffusion and Eurocentric History.* New York.

Boulle, P. H. (1975) 'Marchandises de traite et développement industriel dans la France et l'Angleterre du XVIIIe siècle', *Revue Française Histoire d'Outre-Mer,* 62, 309–30.

Bowen, H. V. (1996) *Elites, Enterprise and the Making of the British Overseas Empire, 1688–1775.*

Breen, T. H. (1986) 'An Empire of Goods: The Anglicization of Colonial America, 1690–1776', *Journal of British Studies,* 25, 467–99.

(1988) ' "Baubles of Britain": The American and Consumer Revolutions of the Eighteenth Century', *Past and Present,* 119, 73–104.

Brewer, J. (1989) *The Sinews of Power: War, Money and the English State, 1688–1783.*

Brewer, J. and Porter, R. (eds.) (1994) *Consumption and the World of Goods.*

Brezis, E. S. (1995) 'Foreign Capital Flows in the Century of Britain's

Industrial Revolution: New Estimates, Controlled Conjectures', *Economic History Review*, 2nd ser., 48, 46–67. Argues that foreign capital flows were important for Britain's industrialisation. Her calculations have been challenged by Nash (1997).

Budka, M. (ed.) (1965) *J. U. Niemcewicz: Under Their Vine and Fig Tree*. Elizabeth, N.J.

Burnard, T. G. (forthcoming) ' "Prodigious Mine": The Wealth of Jamaica Once Again', *Economic History Review*, 2nd ser. An important reassessment of a debate conducted by Sheridan (1965, 1968) and Thomas (1968).

Butler, K. M. (1995) *The Economics of Emancipation: Jamaica and Barbados, 1823–1843*. Chapel Hill, N.C.

Cain, P. J. and Hopkins, A. G. (1993) *British Imperialism: Innovation and Expansion, 1688–1914*.

Carrington, S. H. H. (1984) ' "Econocide": Myth or Reality? The Question of West Indian Decline, 1783–1806' with a reply by S. Drescher, *Boletin de estudios latinoamericanos y del Caribe*, 36, 13–67.

  (1988) *The British West Indies during the American Revolution*. Leiden.

  (1989) 'British West Indian Economic Decline and Abolition, 1775–1807: Revisiting *Econocide*', *Canadian Journal of Latin American and Caribbean Studies*, 14, 33–59.

  (1991) 'The State of the Debate on the Role of Capitalism in the Ending of the Slave System' in H. Beckles and V. A. Shepherd (eds.) *Caribbean Slave Society and Economy: A Student Reader*. Kingston. All of Carrington's pieces follow Williams's lead. For a critique, see McCusker (1997).

Cateau, H. and Carrington, S. H. H. (eds.) (2000) *'Capitalism and Slavery' Fifty Years Later: Eric Eustace Williams – A Reassessment of the Man and his Work*. New York.

Chapman, S. D. (1992) *Merchant Enterprise in Britain: From the Industrial Revolution to World War I*. Cambridge.

Clemens, P. G. E. (1976) 'The Rise of Liverpool, 1665–1750', *Economic History Review*, 2nd ser., 29, 211–25.

Coclanis, P. A. (1989) *The Shadow of a Dream: Economic Life and Death in the South Carolina Low Country, 1670–1920*. Oxford.

  (1990) 'The Wealth of British America on the Eve of Revolution', *Journal of Interdisciplinary History*, 21, 245–60.

Coelho, P. R. P. (1973) 'The Profitability of Imperialism: The British Experience in the West Indies, 1768–1772', *Explorations in Economic History*, 10, 253–80.

Cole, W. A. (1981) 'Factors in Demand' in R. C. Floud and D. N. McCloskey (eds.) *The Economic History of Britain Since 1700*, vol. I, *1700–1860*, 1st edn. Cambridge.

Corfield, P. J. (1982) *The Impact of English Towns 1700–1800*. Oxford.

Crafts, N. F. R. (1985) *British Economic Growth During the Industrial Revolution*. Oxford. The mainstream guide to the subject.

Craton, M. (1974) *Sinews of Empire: A Short History of British Slavery*. New York.

Crossley, D. W. and Saville, R. (eds.) (1991) *The Fuller Letters: Guns, Slaves and Finance, 1728–1755*. Sussex Record Society, vol. 26. Brighton.

Crouzet, F. (1980) 'Toward an Export Economy: British Exports During the Industrial Revolution', *Explorations in Economic History*, 17, 48–93, reprinted as ch. 6 of Crouzet, *Britain Ascendant: Comparative Studies in Franco-British Economic History* (1985). Cambridge.

(1990) 'Angleterre–Brésil, 1697–1850: un siècle et demi d'échanges commerciaux', *Histoire, Economie et Société*, 2, 288–317.

(2000) 'America and the Crisis of the British Imperial Economy, 1803–1807' in McCusker and Morgan (2000).

Crowhurst, R. P. (1977) *The Defence of British Trade, 1689–1815*. Folkestone.

Curtin, P. D. (1969) *The Atlantic Slave Trade: A Census*. Madison, Wis. A pathbreaking synthesis on the volume and direction of the transatlantic slave trade, modified in places but not superseded. A second edition, incorporating revised data, is needed.

(1990) *The Rise and Fall of the Plantation Complex: Essays in Atlantic History*. Cambridge.

Darity, W. A. (1982a) 'A General Equilibrium Model of the Eighteenth-Century Atlantic Slave Trade: A Least-Likely Test for the Caribbean School', *Research in Economic History*, 7, 287–326. This and other articles by Darity tend to support the Williams thesis.

(1982b) 'Mercantilism, Slavery and the Industrial Revolution', *Research in Political Economy*, 5, 1–21.

(1985) 'The Numbers Game and the Profitability of the British Trade in Slaves', *Journal of Economic History*, 45, 693–703.

(1988) 'The Williams Abolition Thesis Before Williams', *Slavery and Abolition*, 9, 29–41.

(1989) 'Profitability of the British Trade in Slaves Once Again', *Explorations in Economic History*, 26, 380–4.

(1992a) 'British Industry and the West Indies Plantations' in J. E. Inikori and S. L. Engerman (eds.) *The Atlantic Slave Trade: Effects on Economies, Societies, and Peoples in Africa, the Americas, and Europe*. Durham, N.C.

(1992b) ' "A Model of Original Sin": Rise of the West and Lag of the Rest', *American Economic Review*, 82, 162–7.

(1998) 'Eric Williams and Slavery: A West Indian Viewpoint', *Callaloo*, 20, 801–16.

(2000) 'Economic Aspects of the British Trade in Slaves: A Fresh Look at the Evidence from the 1789 Report of the Lords of Trade (Committee of Council)' in Cateau and Carrington (2000).

Daunton, M. J. (1995) *Progress and Poverty: An Economic and Social History of Britain, 1700–1850*. Oxford.

Davies, K. G. (1952) 'The Origins of the Commission System in the West India Trade', *Transactions of the Royal Historical Society*, 5th ser., 2, 89–107.

 (1957) *The Royal African Company*.

 (1960–1) 'Essays in Bibliography and Criticism, XLIV, Empire and Capital', *Economic History Review*, 2nd ser., 13, 105–10.

Davis, R. (1954) 'English Foreign Trade, 1660–1700' in Minchinton (1969). Originally published in *Economic History Review*, 2nd ser., 6, 150–66.

 (1962) *The Rise of the English Shipping Industry in the Seventeenth and Eighteenth Centuries*. A book of enduring importance.

 (1962–3) 'English Foreign Trade, 1700–1774', *Economic History Review*, 2nd ser., 15, 285–303, reprinted in Minchinton (1969). A seminal study.

 (1967) *A Commercial Revolution: English Overseas Trade in the Seventeenth and Eighteenth Centuries*.

 (1973) *The Rise of the Atlantic Economies*.

 (1979) *The Industrial Revolution and British Overseas Trade*, Leicester. The best guide to the quantitative dimensions and direction of British foreign trade c. 1780–1850.

Deane, P. and Cole, W. A. (1967) *British Economic Growth 1688–1959: Trends and Structure*, 2nd edn. Cambridge. A very influential text.

Devine, T. M. (1975) *The Tobacco Lords: A Study of the Tobacco Merchants of Glasgow and Their Trading Activities, c. 1740–1790*. Edinburgh.

 (1976) 'The Colonial Trades and Industrial Investment in Scotland, c. 1700–1815', *Economic History Review*, 2nd ser., 29, 1–13.

 (1977) 'Colonial Commerce and the Scottish Economy, c. 1730–1815' in L. M. Cullen and T. C. Smout (eds.) *Comparative Aspects of Scottish and Irish Economic and Social History*. Edinburgh.

 (1978) 'An Eighteenth-Century Business Elite: Glasgow–West India Merchants, c. 1750–1815', *Scottish Historical Review*, 67, 40–67.

Devine, T. M. and Jackson, G. (eds.) (1995) *Glasgow*, vol. I, *Beginnings to 1830*. Manchester.

'Dicky Sam' (1884) *Liverpool and Slavery: An Historical Account of the Liverpool–African Slave Trade*. Liverpool.

Doerflinger, T. M. (1986) *A Vigorous Spirit of Enterprise: Merchants and Economic Development in Revolutionary Philadelphia*. Chapel Hill, N.C. Despite its title, this book includes perceptive indirect comments on merchants and the beginnings of industrialisation in Britain.

 (1988) 'Farmers and Dry Goods in the Philadelphia Market Area,

1750–1800' in R. Hoffman et al. (eds.) *The Economy of Early America: The Revolutionary Period 1763–1790.* Charlottesville, Va.

Drescher, S. (1977) *Econocide: British Slavery in the Era of Abolition.* Pittsburgh. A much-discussed counterblast to *Capitalism and Slavery.*

   (1986) 'The Decline Thesis of British Slavery since *Econocide*', *Slavery and Abolition,* 7, 3–24.

   (1987) 'Eric Williams: British Capitalism and British Slavery', *History and Theory,* 26, 180–96.

   (1997) '*Capitalism and Slavery*: After Fifty Years', *Slavery and Abolition,* 18, 212–27.

Duffy, M. (1987) *Soldiers, Sugar, and Seapower: The British Expeditions to the West Indies and the War Against Revolutionary France.* Oxford.

Dumbell, S. (1931) 'The Profits of the Guinea Trade', *Economic History,* 2, 254–7.

Edwards, M. M. (1967) *The Growth of the British Cotton Trade, 1780–1815.* Manchester.

Elder, M. (1992) *The Slave Trade and the Economic Development of Eighteenth-Century Lancaster.* Halifax.

Eltis, D. (1987) *Economic Growth and the Ending of the Transatlantic Slave Trade.* Oxford.

   (1997) 'The Slave Economies of the Caribbean: Structure, Performance, Evolution and Significance' in F. W. Knight (ed.) *General History of the Caribbean,* vol. III, *The Slave Societies of the Caribbean.*

   (2000) *The Rise of African Slavery in the Americas.* Cambridge.

Eltis, D. and Engerman, S. L. (2000) 'The Importance of Slavery and the Slave Trade to Industrializing Britain', *Journal of Economic History,* 60, 123–44.

Engerman, S. L. (1972) 'The Slave Trade and British Capital Formation in the Eighteenth Century: A Comment on the Williams Thesis', *Business History Review,* 46, 430–43.

   (1975) 'Comments on Richardson and Boulle and the "Williams Thesis"', *Revue Française d'Histoire d'Outre-Mer,* 62, 331–6.

   (1994) 'Mercantilism and Overseas Trade, 1700–1800' in Floud and McCloskey (1994), vol. I, *1700–1860.*

   (1995) 'The Atlantic Economy of the Eighteenth Century: Some Speculations on Economic Development in Britain, America, Africa and Elsewhere', *Journal of European Economic History,* 24, 145–69.

   (1996) 'Europe, the Lesser Antilles, and Economic Expansion, 1600–1800' in R. L. Paquette and S. L. Engerman (eds.) *The Lesser Antilles in the Age of European Expansion.* Gainesville, Fla.

   (1998) 'British Imperialism in a Mercantilist Age, 1492–1849: Conceptual Issues and Empirical Problems', *Revista de Historia Económica,* 16, 195–231.

Esteban, J. Cuenca (1997) 'The Rising Share of British Industrial Exports in Industrial Output, 1700–1851', *Journal of Economic History*, 57, 879–906.

Eversley, D. E. C. (1967) 'The Home Market and Economic Growth in England, 1750–1780' in E. L. Jones and G. E. Mingay (eds.) *Land, Labour and Population in the Industrial Revolution: Essays Presented to J. D. Chambers*. Much-cited article on the value of the home market in the mid-eighteenth century.

Farnie, D. A. (1962–3) 'The Commercial Empire of the Atlantic, 1607–1783', *Economic History Review*, 2nd ser., 15, 205–18.

Fisher, H. E. S. (1971) *The Portugal Trade: A Study of Anglo-Portuguese Commerce 1700–1770*.

(1981) 'Lisbon, Its English Merchant Community and the Mediterranean in the Eighteenth Century' in P. L. Cottrell and D. H. Aldcroft (eds.) *Shipping, Trade and Commerce: Essays in Memory of Ralph Davis*. Leicester.

Flinn, M. W. (1966) *The Origins of the Industrial Revolution*.

Floud, R. C. and McCloskey, D. N. (eds.) (1994) *The Economic History of Britain Since 1700*, 2nd edn. Cambridge.

French, C. J. (1992) ' "Crowded with Traders and a Great Commerce": London's Dominion of English Overseas Trade, 1700–1775', *London Journal*, 17, 27–35.

Green, W. A. (1976) *British Slave Emancipation: The Sugar Colonies and the Great Experiment 1830–1865*. Oxford.

Habakkuk, H. J. and Deane, P. (1963) 'The Take-Off in Britain' in W. W. Rostow (ed.) *The Economics of Take-Off into Sustained Growth*.

Hancock, D. (1995) *Citizens of the World: London Merchants and the Integration of the British Atlantic Community, 1735–1785*. Cambridge.

(2000) 'A Revolution in the Trade: Wine Distribution and the Development of the Infrastructure of the Atlantic Market Economy, 1703–1807' in McCusker and Morgan (2000).

Harding, R. (1995) *The Evolution of the Sailing Navy, 1509–1815*.

Harper, L. A. (1939) *The English Navigation Laws: A Seventeenth-Century Experiment in Social Engineering*. New York.

Hatton, T. J., Lyons, J. S. and Satchell, S. E. (1983) 'Eighteenth-Century British Trade: Homespun or Empire Made?', *Explorations in Economic History*, 20, 163–82.

Higman, B. W. (1996) 'Economic and Social Development of the British West Indies, from Settlement to c. 1850' in S. L. Engerman and R. E. Gallman (eds.) *The Cambridge Economic History of the United States*, vol. I, *The Colonial Era*. Cambridge.

(1999) *Writing West Indian Histories*. Basingstoke.

Hobsbawm, E. J. (1968) *Industry and Empire: An Economic History of Britain Since 1750*.

Hoppit, J. (1987) *Risk and Failure in English Business, 1700–1800*. Cambridge.

Hudson, P. (1992) *The Industrial Revolution*.

Hyde, F. E. (1971) *Liverpool and the Mersey: An Economic History of a Port, 1700–1970*. Newton Abbot.

Hyde, F. E., Parkinson, B. B. and Marriner, S. (1952–3) 'The Nature and Profitability of the Liverpool Slave Trade', *Economic History Review*, 2nd ser., 5, 368–77.

Inikori, J. E. (1981) 'Market Structure and the Profits of the British African Trade in the Late Eighteenth Century', *Journal of Economic History*, 41, 745–76. The claims of this article are critically assessed by Anderson and Richardson (1983, 1985).

(1983) 'Market Structure and the Profits of the British African Trade in the Late Eighteenth Century: A Rejoinder', *Journal of Economic History*, 43, 723–8.

(1987) 'Slavery and the Development of Industrial Capitalism in England' in Solow and Engerman (1987). This and Inikori's other articles strongly support the Williams thesis.

(1990) 'The Credit Needs of the African Trade and the Development of the Credit Economy in England', *Explorations in Economic History*, 27, 197–231.

(1992) 'Slavery and the Revolution in Cotton Textile Production in England' in J. E. Inikori and S. L. Engerman (eds.) *The Atlantic Slave Trade: Effects on Economies, Societies, and Peoples in Africa, the Americas and Europe*. Durham, N.C.

(1993) *Slavery and the Rise of Capitalism*. Mona, Jamaica. The 1993 Elsa Goveia Memorial Lecture.

(2000) '*Capitalism and Slavery*, Fifty Years After: Eric Williams and the Changing Explanations of the Industrial Revolution' in Cateau and Carrington (2000).

Jackson, G. (1983) 'The Ports' in D. H. Aldcroft and M. J. Freeman (eds.) *Transport in the Industrial Revolution*. Manchester.

James, C. L. R. (1983) *The Black Jacobins: Toussaint l'Ouverture and the San Domingo Revolution*.

John, A. H. (1958) 'The London Assurance Company and the Marine Insurance Market of the Eighteenth Century', *Economica*, ns, 25, 126–41.

(1965) 'Agricultural Productivity and Economic Growth in England, 1700–1760', *Journal of Economic History*, 25, 19–34.

Jones, D. W. (1988) *War and Economy in the Age of William III and Marlborough*. Oxford.

Kindleberger, C. P. (1975) 'Commercial Expansion and the Industrial Revolution', *Journal of European Economic History*, 4, 613–54.

Klein, H. S. (1990) 'Economic Aspects of the Eighteenth-Century Atlantic

Slave Trade' in J. D. Tracy (ed.) *The Rise of Merchant Empires: Long-Distance Trade in the Early Modern World 1350–1750*. Cambridge.

(1999) *The Atlantic Slave Trade*. Cambridge.

Langton, J. (1983) 'Liverpool and Its Hinterland in the Late Eighteenth Century' in B. L. Anderson and P. J. M. Stoney (eds.) *Commerce, Industry and Transport: Studies in Economic Change on Merseyside*. Liverpool.

Lee, C. H. (1986) *The British Economy Since 1700: A Macroeconomic Perspective*. Cambridge.

McCloskey, D. N. (1994) '1780–1860: A Survey' in Floud and McCloskey (1994), vol. I, *1700–1860*.

McCusker, J. J. (1978) *Money and Exchange in Europe and America, 1600–1775: A Handbook*. Chapel Hill, N.C.

(1996) 'British Mercantilist Policies and the American Colonies' in S. L. Engerman and R. E. Gallman (eds.) *The Cambridge Economic History of the United States*, vol. I, *The Colonial Era*. Cambridge.

(1997) *Essays in the Economic History of the Atlantic World.*

McCusker, J. J. and Menard, R. R. (1985) *The Economy of British America, 1607–1789*. Chapel Hill, N.C. An indispensable vade-mecum to the economic history of colonial North America, with an excellent bibliographical guide to publications in that field. A reprinted edition (1991) includes an updated bibliography.

McCusker, J. J. and Morgan, K. (eds.) (2000) *The Early Modern Atlantic Economy*. Cambridge.

McDonald, R. A. (1979) 'The Williams Thesis: A Comment on the State of Scholarship', *Caribbean Quarterly*, 25, 63–8.

McFarlane, A. (1994) *The British in the Americas 1480–1815*.

McKendrick, N., Brewer, J. and Plumb, J. H. (1983) *The Birth of a Consumer Society: The Commercialization of Eighteenth-Century England*. The major statement on the 'consumer revolution' of eighteenth-century Britain.

Malthus, T. R. (1826) *An Essay on the Principle of Population*, 6th edn.

Marshall, P. J. (ed.) (1998) *The Oxford History of the British Empire*, vol. II, *The Eighteenth Century*. Oxford.

Mathias, P. (1983) *The First Industrial Nation: An Economic History of Britain, 1700–1914*, 2nd edn.

(2000) 'Risk, Credit and Kinship in Early Modern Enterprise' in McCusker and Morgan (2000).

Menard, R. R. (1998) 'Reckoning with Williams: *Capitalism and Slavery* and the Reconstruction of Early American History', *Callaloo*, 20, 791–9.

Minchinton, W. E. (1954) 'Bristol – Metropolis of the West in the Eighteenth Century', *Transactions of the Royal Historical Society*, 5th ser., 4, 69–89.

(ed.) (1969) *The Growth of English Overseas Trade in the Seventeenth and Eighteenth Centuries.*

(1983) 'Williams and Drescher: Abolition and Emancipation', *Slavery and Abolition*, 4, 81–105.

(1996) 'Abolition and Emancipation: Williams, Drescher and the Continuing Debate' in R. A. McDonald (ed.) *West Indies Accounts: Essays on the History of the British Caribbean and the Atlantic Economy in Honour of Richard Sheridan*. Mona, Jamaica.

Mirowski, P. (1982) 'Adam Smith, Empiricism, and the Rate of Profit in Eighteenth-Century England', *History of Political Economy*, 5, 178–98.

Morgan, K. (ed.) (1992) *An American Quaker in the British Isles: The Travel Journals of Jabez Maud Fisher, 1775–1779*. Oxford.

(1993a) *Bristol and the Atlantic Trade in the Eighteenth Century*. Cambridge.

(1993b) 'Bristol West India Merchants in the Eighteenth Century', *Transactions of the Royal Historical Society*, 6th ser., 3, 185–208.

(1996a) 'Atlantic Trade and British Economic Growth in the Eighteenth Century' in P. Mathias and J. A. Davis (eds.) *The Nature of Industrialization: International Trade and British Economic Growth Since the Eighteenth Century*. Oxford.

(1996b) 'The Economic Development of Bristol, 1700–1850' in M. Dresser and P. Ollerenshaw (eds.) *The Making of Modern Bristol*. Tiverton.

(1998) 'Sugar Refining in Bristol' in K. Bruland and P. K. O'Brien (eds.) *From Family Firms to Corporate Capitalism: Essays in Business and Industrial History in Honour of Peter Mathias*. Oxford.

(2000a) 'Business Networks in the British Export Trade to North America, 1750–1800' in McCusker and Morgan (2000).

(2000b) 'The Impact of Slavery and Atlantic Trade on the British Economy, 1660–1800' in H. Pietschmann (ed.) *History of the Atlantic System (c. 1580–c. 1830)*. Transactions of the Joachim Jungius–Gesellschaft der Wissenschaften. Göttingen.

Morgan, P. D. (1998) 'The Black Experience in the British Empire, 1680–1810' in Marshall (1998).

Nash, R. C. (1982) 'The English and Scottish Tobacco Trades in the Seventeenth and Eighteenth Centuries: Legal and Illegal Trade', *Economic History Review*, 2nd ser., 35, 354–72.

(1985) 'Irish Atlantic Trade in the Seventeenth and Eighteenth Centuries', *William and Mary Quarterly*, 3rd ser., 42, 329–56.

(1992) 'South Carolina and the Atlantic Economy in the Late Seventeenth and Eighteenth Centuries', *Economic History Review*, 2nd ser., 45, 677–702.

(1997) 'The Balance of Payments and Foreign Capital Flows in Eighteenth-Century England: A Comment', *Economic History Review*, 2nd ser., 50, 110–28. Corrects many of the figures provided by Brezis

(1995) and argues against her view that foreign capital flows were important for Britain's industrialisation.

Neal, L. (1994) 'The Finance of Business During the Industrial Revolution' in Floud and McCloskey (1994), vol. I, *1700–1860*.

O'Brien, P. K. (1982) 'European Economic Development: The Contribution of the Periphery', *Economic History Review*, 2nd ser., 35, 1–18. Wide-ranging and provocative.

(1985) 'Agriculture and the Home Market for English Industry, 1660–1820', *English Historical Review*, 100, 773–800.

(1990) 'European Industrialisation: From the Voyages of Discovery to the Industrial Revolution' in H. Pohl (ed.) *The European Discovery of the World and Its Economic Effects on Pre-Industrial Society, 1500–1800.* Stuttgart.

(1994) 'Central Government and the Economy, 1688–1815' in Floud and McCloskey (1994), vol. I, *1700–1860*.

(1998) 'Inseparable Connections: Trade, Economy, Fiscal State, and the Expansion of Empire, 1688–1815' in Marshall (1998).

O'Brien, P. K. and Engerman, S. L. (1991) 'Exports and the Growth of the British Economy from the Glorious Revolution to the Peace of Amiens' in Solow (1991).

O'Brien, P. K. and de la Escosura, L. P. (1998) 'The Costs and Benefits for Europeans from Their Empires Overseas', *Revista de Historia Económica*, 16, 29–89.

Ormrod, D. (1984) 'English Re-exports and the Dutch Staple Market in the Eighteenth Century' in D. C. Coleman and P. Mathias (eds.) *Enterprise and History: Essays in Honour of Charles Wilson.* Cambridge.

(1993) 'The Atlantic Economy and the "Protestant Capitalist International", 1651–1775', *Historical Research*, 66, 197–208.

O'Shaughnessy, A. (2000) 'Eric Williams as Economic Historian' in Cateau and Carrington (2000).

Palmer, C. A. (1981) *Human Cargoes: The British Slave Trade to Spanish America, 1700–1739.* Urbana, Ill.

Pares, R. (1936) *War and Trade in the West Indies, 1739–1763.* Oxford.

(1936–7) 'The Economic Factors in the History of the Empire', *Economic History Review*, 7, 119–44.

(1950) *A West-India Fortune.*

(1956) *Yankees and Creoles: The Trade Between North America and the West Indies Before the American Revolution.* New York.

(1960) *Merchants and Planters, Economic History Review*, supplement no. 4. Cambridge.

Parkinson, B. B. (1951) 'A Slaver's Accounts', *Accounting Research*, 2, 144–50.

Pitman, F. W. (1917) *The Development of the British West Indies, 1700–1763.* New Haven, Conn.

(1931) 'The Settlement and Financing of British West India Plantations in the Eighteenth Century' in *Essays in Colonial History Presented to Charles McLean Andrews by His Students*. New Haven, Conn.

Price, J. M. (1954) 'The Rise of Glasgow in the Chesapeake Tobacco Trade, 1700–1775', *William and Mary Quarterly*, 3rd ser., 11, 179–99. Reprinted in Price (1995).

(1973) *France and the Chesapeake: A History of the French Tobacco Monopoly, 1674–1791, and of Its Relationship to the British and American Tobacco Trades*, 2 vols. Ann Arbor, Mich.

(1979) 'Colonial Trade and British Economic Development, 1660–1775' in *La Révolution Américaine et l'Europe*, Colloques internationaux du Centre Nationale de la Recherche Scientifique, no. 577. Paris. Reprinted in Price (1996c).

(1980) *Capital and Credit in British Overseas Trade: The View from the Chesapeake, 1700–1776*. Cambridge, Mass.

(1984) 'The Transatlantic Economy' in J. P. Greene and J. R. Pole (eds.) *Colonial British America: Essays in the New History of the Early Modern Era*. Baltimore. Reprinted in Price (1996a).

(1989) 'What Did Merchants Do?: Reflections on British Overseas Trade, 1660–1790', *Journal of Economic History*, 49, 267–84. Reprinted in Price (1996c).

(1991) 'Credit in the Slave Trade and Plantation Economies' in Solow (1991). Reprinted in Price (1996a).

(1992) *Perry of London: A Family and a Firm on the Seaborne Frontier, 1615–1753*. Cambridge, Mass.

(1995) *Tobacco in Atlantic Trade: The Chesapeake, London and Glasgow, 1675–1775*. Aldershot.

(1996a) *The Atlantic Frontier of the Thirteen American Colonies and States: Essays in Eighteenth-Century Commercial and Social History*. Aldershot.

(1996b) 'Competition Between Ports in British Long Distance Trade, c. 1660–1800' in A. Guimera and D. Romero (eds.) *Puertos y sistemas portuarios (siglos XVI–XX)*. Madrid.

(1996c) *Overseas Trade and Traders: Essays on Some Commercial, Financial and Political Challenges Facing British Atlantic Merchants, 1660–1775*. Aldershot.

(1998) 'The Imperial Economy, 1700–1776' in Marshall (1998).

Price, J. M. and Clemens, P. G. E. (1987) 'A Revolution of Scale in Overseas Trade: British Firms in the Chesapeake Trade, 1675–1775', *Journal of Economic History*, 47, 1–43. Reprinted in Price (1995).

Ragatz, L. J. (1928) *The Fall of the Planter Class in the British Caribbean, 1763–1833*. New York. The pioneer work that argued for a decline in the West Indian plantation economy after the Seven Years War.

Ramsay, G. D. (1957) *English Overseas Trade During the Centuries of*

Emergence: Studies in Some Modern Origins of the English-Speaking World.

Rawley, J. A. (1981) *The Trans-Atlantic Slave Trade.* New York.

Raynal, Abbé (1788) *A Philosophical . . . History . . . of the East and West Indies.*

Richardson, D. (1975) 'Profitability in the Bristol–Liverpool Slave Trade', *Revue Française d'Histoire d'Outre-Mer*, 62, 301–6.

(1976) 'Profits in the Liverpool Slave Trade: The Accounts of William Davenport, 1757–1784' in R. Anstey and P. E. H. Hair (eds.) *Liverpool, the African Slave Trade, and Abolition.* Historic Society of Lancashire and Cheshire, Occasional Series, vol. 2.

(1985) *The Bristol Slave Traders: A Collective Portrait.* Bristol.

(1986) *Bristol, Africa, and the Eighteenth-Century Slave Trade to America*, vol. I, *The Years of Expansion 1698–1729.* Bristol.

(1987a) 'The Costs of Survival: The Transport of Slaves in the Middle Passage and the Profitability of the Eighteenth-Century British Slave Trade', *Explorations in Economic History*, 24, 178–96. One of several articles by Richardson that provide critiques of the evidence and methodology deployed in Darity's and Inikori's articles on the British slave trade.

(1987b) 'The Slave Trade, Sugar, and British Economic Growth, 1748–1776', *Journal of Interdisciplinary History*, 17, 739–69, reprinted in Solow and Engerman (1987).

(1989a) 'Accounting for Profits in the British Trade in Slaves: Reply to William Darity', *Explorations in Economic History*, 26, 492–9.

(1989b) 'The Eighteenth-Century British Slave Trade: Estimates of its Volume and Coastal Distribution in Africa' in P. Uselding (ed.) *Research in Economic History*, 12, 151–95.

(1991) 'Slavery, Trade, and Economic Growth in Eighteenth-Century New England' in Solow (1991).

(1994) 'Liverpool and the English Slave Trade' in A. Tibbles (ed.) *Transatlantic Slavery: Against Human Dignity.*

(ed.) (1996) *Bristol, Africa and the Eighteenth-Century Slave Trade to America*, vol. IV, *The Final Years, 1770–1807.* Bristol.

(1998) 'The British Empire and the Atlantic Slave Trade, 1660–1807' in Marshall (1998).

Richardson, D. and Evans, E. W. (1996) 'Empire and Accumulation in Eighteenth-Century Britain' in T. Brotherstone and G. Pilling (eds.) *History, Economic History and the Future of Marxism: Essays in Memory of Tom Kemp.*

Richardson, P. (1968) *Empire and Slavery.*

Robinson, C. J. (1987) 'Capitalism, Slavery and Bourgeois Historiography', *History Workshop: A Journal of Socialist and Feminist Historians*, 23, 122–40. A provocative, but diffuse, defence of *Capitalism and Slavery.*

Rodger, N. A. M. (1998) 'Sea Power and Empire, 1688–1793' in Marshall (1998).

Roseveare, H. G. (1996) 'The Eighteenth-Century Port of London Reconsidered' in A. Guimera and D. Romero (eds.) *Puertos y sistemas portuarios (siglos XVI–XX)*. Madrid.

(2000) 'Property Versus Commerce in the mid-Eighteenth-Century Port of London', in McCusker and Morgan (2000).

Ryden, D. (2001) 'Does Decline Make Sense? The Economy of the British West Indies and Abolition, 1750–1807', *Journal of Interdisciplinary History*.

Schumpeter, E. B. (1960) *English Overseas Trade Statistics, 1697–1808*, Oxford. An essential reference source.

Shammas, C. (1990) *The Pre-Industrial Consumer in England and America*. Oxford.

Shepherd, J. F. and Walton, G. M. (1972) *Shipping, Maritime Trade, and the Economic Development of Colonial North America*. Cambridge.

Sheridan, R. B. (1958) 'The Commercial and Financial Organisation of the British Slave Trade, 1750–1807', *Economic History Review*, 2nd ser., 11, 249–63.

(1964) 'Planter and Historian: The Career of William Beckford of Jamaica and England, 1744–1799', *Jamaican Historical Review*, 4, 36–58.

(1965) 'The Wealth of Jamaica in the Eighteenth Century', *Economic History Review*, 2nd ser., 18, 292–311.

(1968) 'The Wealth of Jamaica in the Eighteenth Century: A Rejoinder', *Economic History Review*, 2nd ser., 21, 46–61.

(1969) 'The Plantation Revolution and the Industrial Revolution, 1625–1775', *Caribbean Studies*, 9, 5–25.

(1973) *Sugar and Slavery: An Economic History of the British West Indies 1623–1775*. Baltimore. Still the best book-length economic treatment of the British Caribbean before the American Revolution.

Smail, J. (1999) *Merchants, Markets and Manufacture: The English Wool Textile Industry in the Eighteenth Century*.

Smith, S. D. (1995) 'British Exports to Colonial North America and the Mercantilist Fallacy', *Business History*, 37, 45–63.

(1998) 'The Market for Manufactures in the Thirteen Continental Colonies, 1698–1776', *Economic History Review*, 2nd ser., 51, 676–708.

Solow, B. L. (1985) 'Caribbean Slavery and British Growth: The Eric Williams Hypothesis', *Journal of Development Economics*, 17, 99–115. Forthright support for the Williams thesis.

(1987) 'Capitalism and Slavery in the Exceedingly Long Run' in Solow and Engerman (1987).

(ed.) (1991) *Slavery and the Rise of the Atlantic System*. Cambridge.

Solow, B. L. and Engerman, S. L. (eds.) (1987) *British Capitalism and Caribbean Slavery: The Legacy of Eric Williams*. Includes some important reassessments of *Capitalism and Slavery*.

Starkey, D. J. (1990) *British Privateering Enterprise in the Eighteenth Century*. Exeter.

Steele, I. K. (1986) *The English Atlantic, 1675–1740: An Exploration of Communication and Community*. Oxford.

Supple, B. E. (1970) *The Royal Exchange Assurance: A History of British Insurance 1720–1970*. Cambridge.

Thomas, R. P. (1968) 'The Sugar Colonies of the Old Empire: Profit or Loss for Great Britain?', *Economic History Review*, 2nd ser., 21, 30–45.

Thomas, R. P. and Bean, R. N. (1974) 'The Fishers of Men: The Profits of the Slave Trade', *Journal of Economic History*, 34, 885–914.

Thomas, R. P. and McCloskey, D. N. (1981) 'Overseas Trade and Empire, 1700–1860' in R. C. Floud and D. N. McCloskey (eds.) *The Economic History of Britain Since 1700*, vol. I, *1700–1860*, 1st edn. Cambridge.

Trebilcock, R. C. (1985) *Phoenix Assurance and the Development of British Insurance*, vol. I, *1782–1870*. Cambridge.

Truxes, T. M. (1988) *Irish–American Trade, 1660–1783*. Cambridge.

Wadsworth, A. P. and Mann, J. de L. (1931) *The Cotton Trade and Industrial Lancashire, 1600–1780*. Manchester.

Wallace, James (1795) *A General and Descriptive History of the Ancient and Present State of the Town of Liverpool*. Liverpool.

Wallerstein, I. (1980) *The Modern World System*, vol. II, *Mercantilism and the Consolidation of the European World Economy 1600–1750*. New York. A Marxist treatment of broad themes.

Walton, G. M. and Shepherd, J. F. (1979) *The Economic Rise of Early America*. Cambridge.

Walvin, J. (1993) *Black Ivory: A History of British Slavery*.

(1997) *Fruits of Empire: Exotic Produce and British Taste, 1660–1800*.

Ward, J. R. (1978) 'The Profitability of Sugar Planting in the British West Indies, 1650–1834', *Economic History Review*, 2nd ser., 31, 197–213.

(1985) *Poverty and Progress in the Caribbean 1800–1960*.

(1988) *British West Indian Slavery: The Process of Amelioration, 1750–1834*. Oxford.

(1998) 'The British West Indies in the Age of Abolition, 1748–1815' in Marshall (1998).

Williams, E. (1944) *Capitalism and Slavery*. Chapel Hill, N.C. Still a seminal book even though its insights and evidence are much contested.

(1964) *British Historians and the West Indies*. Port-of-Spain, Trinidad.

(1970) *From Columbus to Castro: The History of the Caribbean 1492–1969*.

Williams, G. (1897) *History of the Liverpool Privateers and Letters of Marque with an Account of the Liverpool Slave Trade.*

Williams, W. E. (1938) *Africa and the Rise of Capitalism.* Howard University Studies in the Social Sciences, vol. 1. Washington, D.C.

Wilson, R. G. (1973) 'The Supremacy of the Yorkshire Cloth Industry in the Eighteenth Century' in N. B. Harte and K. G. Ponting (eds.) *Textile History and Economic History: Essays in Honour of Miss Julia de Lacy Mann.* Manchester.

Wright, C. and Fayle, C. E. (1928) *A History of Lloyd's.*

Zahedieh, N. B. (1994) 'London and the Colonial Consumer in the Late Seventeenth Century', *Economic History Review*, 2nd ser., 47, 239–61.

    (1998a) 'Credit, Risk and Reputation in British Atlantic Trade in the Seventeenth Century' in O. Janzen (ed.) *Merchant Organization and Maritime Trades, Research in Maritime History*, 15 (special issue), 53–74.

    (1998b) 'Overseas Expansion and Trade in the Seventeenth Century' in N. P. Canny (ed.) *The Oxford History of the British Empire*, vol. I, *The Origins of Empire: British Overseas Enterprise to the Close of the Seventeenth Century.* Oxford.

    (1999) 'Making Mercantilism Work: London Merchants and Atlantic Trade in the Seventeenth Century', *Transactions of the Royal Historical Society*, 6th ser., 9, 143–58.

Index

New Studies in Economic and Social History

Titles in the series available from Cambridge University Press

12. M. Collins, *Banks and Industrial Finance, 1800–1939*
    ISBN 0 521 55271 0 (hardback) 0 521 55782 8 (paperback)
13. A. Dyer, *Decline and Growth in English Towns, 1400–1640*
    ISBN 0 521 55272 9 (hardback) 0 521 55781 X (paperback)
14. R. B. Outhwaite *Dearth, Public Policy and Social Disturbance in England, 1550–1800*
    ISBN 0 521 55273 7 (hardback) 0 521 55780 1 (paperback)
15. M. Sanderson, *Education, Economic Change and Society in England 1780–1870* (second edition)
    ISBN 0 521 55274 5 (hardback) 0 521 55779 8 (paperback)
16. R. D. Anderson, *Universities and Elites in Britain since 1800*
    ISBN 0 521 55275 3 (hardback) 0 521 55778 X (paperback)
17. C. Heywood, *The Development of the French Economy, 1700–1914*
    ISBN 0 521 55276 1 (hardback) 0 521 55777 1 (paperback)
18. R. A. Houston, *The Population History of Britain and Ireland, 1500–1750*
    ISBN 0 521 55277 X (hardback) 0 521 55776 3 (paperback)
19. A. J. Reid, *Social Classes and Social Relations in Britain, 1850–1914*
    ISBN 0 521 55278 8 (hardback) 0 521 55775 5 (paperback)
20. R. Woods, *The Population of Britain in the Nineteenth Century*
    ISBN 0 521 55279 6 (hardback) 0 521 55774 7 (paperback)
21. T. C. Barker, *The Rise and Rise of Road Transport, 1700–1990*
    ISBN 0 521 55280 X (hardback) 0 521 55773 9 (paperback)
22. J. Harrison, *The Spanish Economy*
    ISBN 0 521 55281 8 (hardback) 0 521 55772 0 (paperback)
23. C. Schmitz, *The Growth of Big Business in the United States and Western Europe, 1850–1939*
    ISBN 0 521 55282 6 (hardback) 0 521 55771 2 (paperback)
24. R. A. Church, *The Rise and Decline of the British Motor Industry*
    ISBN 0 521 55283 4 (hardback) 0 521 55770 4 (paperback)
25. P. Horn, *Children's Work and Welfare, 1780–1880*
    ISBN 0 521 55284 2 (hardback) 0 521 55769 0 (paperback)
26. R. Perren, *Agriculture in Depression, 1870–1940*
    ISBN 0 521 55285 0 (hardback) 0 521 55768 2 (paperback)
27. R. J. Overy, *The Nazi Economic Recovery, 1932–1939* (second edition)
    ISBN 0 521 55286 9 (hardback) 0 521 55767 4 (paperback)

28. S. Cherry, *Medical Services and the Hospitals in Britain, 1860–1939*
    ISBN 0 521 57126 X (hardback) 0 521 57784 5 (paperback)
29. D. Edgerton, *Science, Technology and the British Industrial 'Decline',
    1870–1970*
    ISBN 0 521 57127 8 (hardback) 0 521 57778 0 (paperback)
30. C. A. Whatley, *The Industrial Revolution in Scotland*
    ISBN 0 521 57228 2 (hardback) 0 521 57643 1 (paperback)
31. H. E. Meller, *Towns, Plans and Society in Modern Britain*
    ISBN 0 521 57227 4 (hardback) 0 521 57644 X (paperback)
32. H. Hendrick, *Children, Childhood and English Society, 1880–1990*
    ISBN 0 521 57253 3 (hardback) 0 521 57000 0 (paperback)
33. N. Tranter, *Sport, Economy and Society in Britain, 1750–1914*
    ISBN 0 521 57217 7 (hardback) 0 521 57655 5 (paperback)
34. R. W. Davies, *Soviet Economic Development from Lenin to Khrushchev*
    ISBN 0 521 66260 3 (hardback) 0 521 62742 7 (paperback)
35. H. V. Bowen, *War and British Society, 1688–1815*
    ISBN 0 521 57226 6 (hardback) 0 521 57645 8 (paperback)
36. M. M. Smith, *Debating Slavery: Economy and Society in the Antebellum
    American South*
    ISBN 0 521 57158 8 (hardback) 0 521 57696 2 (paperback)
37. M. Sanderson, *Education and Economic Decline in Britain, 1870 to the
    1990s*
    ISBN 0 521 58170 2 (hardback) 0 521 58842 1 (paperback)
38. V. Berridge, *Health Policy, Health and Society, 1939 to the 1990s*
    ISBN 0 521 57230 4 (hardback) 0 521 57641 5 (paperback)
39. M. E. Mate, *Women in Medieval English Society*
    ISBN 0 521 58322 5 (hardback) 0 521 58733 6 (paperback)
40. P. J. Richardson, *Economic Change in China, c. 1800–1950*
    ISBN 0 521 58396 9 (hardback) 0 521 63571 3 (paperback)
41. J. E. Archer, *Social Unrest and Popular Protest in England, 1780–1840*
    ISBN 0 521 57216 9 (hardback) 0 521 57656 3 (paperback)
42. K. Morgan, *Slavery, Atlantic Trade and the British Economy,
    1660–1800*
    ISBN 0 521 58213 X (hardback) 0 521 58814 6 (paperback)
43. C. W. Chalklin, *The Rise of the English Town, 1650–1850*
    ISBN 0 521 66141 2 (hardback) 0 521 66737 2 (paperback)

Previously published as

Studies in Economic and Social History

Titles in the series available from the Macmillan Press Limited:

Economic History Society

The Economic History Society, which numbers around 3,000 members, publishes the quarterly *Economic History Review* (free to members) and holds an annual conference. Enquiries about membership should be addressed to The Assistant Secretary, Economic History Society, PO Box 70, Kingswood, Bristol BS15 5TB. Full-time students may join at special rates.